Snorkeling Florida

UNIVERSITY PRESS OF FLORIDA

Florida A&M University, Tallahassee
Florida Atlantic University, Boca Raton
Florida Gulf Coast University, Ft. Myers
Florida International University, Miami
Florida State University, Tallahassee
New College of Florida, Sarasota
University of Central Florida, Orlando
University of Florida, Gainesville
University of North Florida, Jacksonville
University of South Florida, Tampa
University of West Florida, Pensacola

University Press of Florida

Gainesville

Tallahassee

Tampa

Boca Raton

Pensacola

Orlando

Miami

Jacksonville

Ft. Myers

Sarasota

Snorkeling Florida

50 Excellent Sites

Brad Bertelli

Copyright 2008 by Brad Bertelli
Printed in the United States of America on acid-free paper
All rights reserved

13 12 11 10 09 08   6 5 4 3 2 1

Library of Congress Cataloging-in-Publication Data
Bertelli, Brad.
Snorkeling Florida : 50 excellent sites / Brad Bertelli.
p. cm.
ISBN 978-0-8130-3275-7 (alk. paper)
1. Skin diving—Florida—Guidebooks. 2. Scuba diving—Florida—
Guidebooks. 3. Florida—Guidebooks. I. Title.
GV840.S78B43 2008
797.2'309759—dc22   2008015554

The University Press of Florida is the scholarly publishing agency
for the State University System of Florida, comprising Florida A&M
University, Florida Atlantic University, Florida Gulf Coast University,
Florida International University, Florida State University, New College
of Florida, University of Central Florida, University of Florida,
University of North Florida, University of South Florida,
and University of West Florida.

University Press of Florida
15 Northwest 15th Street
Gainesville, FL 32611-2079
http://www.upf.com

Contents

Part II. Preparations and Precautions

Snorkeling Florida

Why snorkeling? Unlike scuba diving, snorkeling requires little in-struction and no certification, depth charts, compression tables, or expensive equipment. It is not a physically exacting enterprise and, generally speaking, requires little more exertion than a backyard game of badminton. Compared to scuba diving, snorkeling is a Sunday morning garden stroll.

Why Florida? The Sunshine State boasts 8,462 miles of coastline, seagrass meadows, aquamarine angel fish (Plate 1), sea turtles, dol-phins, sunken ships, Spanish anchors, cannons, and warm, clear water. These treasures, however, represent the mere tip of Florida's snorkeling juggernaut. Intrepid snorkelers can see underwater ho-tels, gin-clear freshwater springs, manatees, and, if they are lucky, flaxen-haired mermaids.

Florida's most alluring feature, however, is coral. Nowhere else in continental North America can snorkelers experience the beautiful wonders of a coral reef. The third-largest barrier reef system in the world grows in the shallow Atlantic waters off Florida's Keys. What makes the coral reefs Florida's number one snorkeling destination, aside from their brilliant hues of red, orange, purple, yellow, and green, are the elaborate systems of nooks and crannies they cre-ate that provide the kinds of structures around which marine life builds communities; coral reefs are magnets for biodiversity.

Corals may be brilliantly colored, but they are not flowers. Do not pick the corals! They are respiring animals called hydrozoans and are related to sea anemones and jellyfish. Corals are a delicate species and snorkelers should make every effort to avoid any and all contact with them.

Swimming fins, a mask, and a snorkel are the three basic pieces of equipment. However, snorkeling is not necessarily about swim-ming. To fully appreciate a snorkeling adventure requires a great

Another beautiful Florida sunset.

deal of floating. Floating over a single spot for a few minutes can reveal more forms of life than would swimming hurriedly past. In a seagrass bed, for instance, what might at first glance appear to be a swaying blade of grass might actually be a seahorse!

The 50 excellent snorkeling sites identified in this guide cover the breadth of the Florida snorkeling experience: freshwater springs and rivers, shipwrecks, seagrass beds, hard-bottom coral communities, coral reefs, and manatees. Each site is rated from Beginner to Advanced and given a full set of particulars including GPS numbers, physical addresses, directions, hours of operation, visitor information, Web sites (when available), and in the Keys, boat ramps.

The physical makeup of each site is described and useful information is offered regarding matters of interest, be they a ballast stone pile from an eighteenth-century Spanish galleon or a particular species of fish or coral to look for. The five areas of the state explored are the Keys, the Southeast Coastline, Springs and Rivers, Panhandle Beaches, and the Southwest Coastline.

The Sunshine State, however, has more to offer snorkelers than snorkeling; it is steeped in local color. Brilliant sunsets aside, Florida offers dead mullet–throwing contests, alligator wrestling, hand-carved coral castles, cracked conch, and Key West. Add a dash of that salty mystique locally referred to as Margaritaville, and it becomes crystal clear why so many Floridians think of home as paradise.

Alphabetical List of Sites

Snorkeling Florida

50 Excellent Sites

Florida

1. Carysfort Reef
2. The Elbow
3. Jules' Undersea Lodge
4. John Pennekamp Coral Reef State Park
5. French Reef
6. Molasses Reef
7. Pickles Reef
8. Conch Reef
9. Founder's Park
10. Hens and Chickens
11. Davis Reef
12. Alligator Reef
13. Indian Key
14. The *San Pedro* Underwater Archeological Preserve State Park
15. Coffins Patch Reef
16. Sombrero Beach
17. Delta Shoals
18. Sombrero Reef
19. Bahia Honda State Park
20. Looe Key
21. Newfound Harbor
22. Key West Marine Park
23. Sand Key
24. The Dry Docks
25. Cottrell Key
26. Marquesas Keys
27. Dry Tortugas
28. Biscayne National Park
29. John U. Lloyd Park
30. Datura Avenue Shipwreck Snorkel Trail
31. Red Reef Park
32. Bathtub Reef Park
33. Fort Pierce Inlet State Park
34. Pepper Beach State Recreational Area
35. Jaycee Park
36. Sebastian Inlet Park
37. Weeki Wachee
38. Crystal River and Homosassa
39. Rainbow Springs State Park
40. Manatee Springs State Park
41. Ginnie Springs
42. Fort Pickens
43. Destin Pass
44. St. Andrews State Recreational Park
45. St. Joseph Peninsula State Park
46. Egmont Key
47. The Sugar Barge
48. Venice Public Beach
49. Cayo Costa State Park
50. Delnor-Wiggins Pass State Park

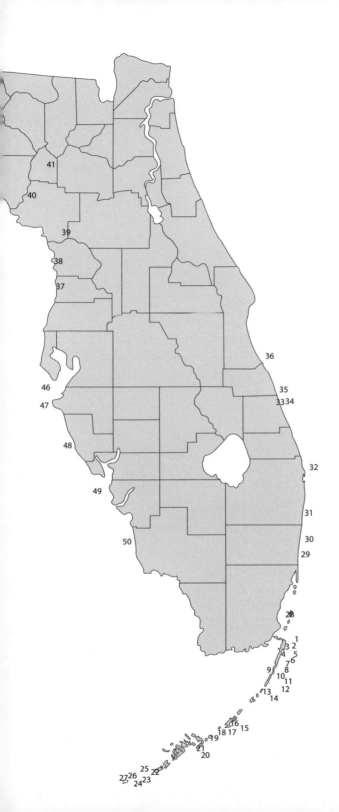

Part I

50 Excellent
Snorkeling Sites

Chapter 1

The Florida Keys

What makes the snorkeling so fantastic in the Keys, besides the clear, warm water, are the coral reefs growing in the shallows of the Atlantic a handful of miles offshore. Corals are a sedentary lot and do not go out foraging for food. Rather, they rely solely on delivery via the sweeping currents of the Gulf Stream of nutrient-rich water.

For the most part, corals are named for the appearance of the structure a particular species creates. A sea fan, for instance, looks like a delicately laced underwater fan. Brain coral appears as intricately grooved as a human brain. These structures are not created by a single coral animal but by colonies of hundreds and sometimes thousands of individual creatures called polyps.

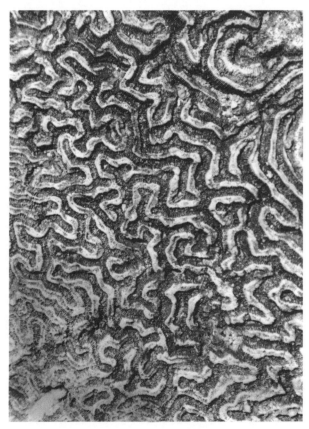

Fossilized brain coral found at Windley Key.

There are two kinds of corals: hard and soft. Hard corals are called stony corals. Soft corals are called octocorals. Both are fantastic colonizers. Though they appear richly hued, corals are a drab species relying on algae called zooanthellae—which live inside the polyps—to lend them color. Corals are basically whitewashed condominium complexes housing zooanthellae—living coats of paint.

For the most part, reefs develop in two different ways—as patch reefs, or as spur-and-groove reefs. Patch reefs grow like an oasis in an underwater desert. Spur-and-groove reef formations have two parts—the spur and the groove. The spurs are a series of coral hedges; the groove is the space between them. These limestone patches, ledges, and crags can be festooned with the green antlers of staghorn corals, sea fans, star corals, or purple sea plumes.

Because Florida's coral reefs are some of the most highly visited in the world, many are protected by the Florida Keys National Marine Sanctuary. Protected reefs are designated as Sanctuary Preservation Areas (SPAs) and are clearly marked by a system of four yellow buoys. Only swimming, snorkeling, and diving are permitted in an SPA. It is illegal to fish, lobster, or harvest any kind of material from an SPA—dead or alive. Whenever snorkeling over the reefs, try to keep in mind that you're engaged in a hands-off activity. Corals are a delicate species and as a responsible snorkeler, you should make every effort not to touch them with your hands or fins. (Picture a coral reef as downtown Tokyo and yourself as Godzilla. Be a careful monster.)

Corals, like angelfish and lobster, are not relegated to the reefs found offshore. In fact, it is possible to find corals close to shore. These hard-bottom coral communities can grow within swimming distance from shore, and while they may not be as significant as the reefs offshore, they can be as breathtaking as wildflowers.

Seagrass beds are also prevalent snorkeling environments. These emerald meadows do not immediately appear to teem with life because the inhabitants are doing their best to blend in. Patient snorkelers willing to explore these beds may see fingernail-sized versions of fish commonly found on the reef as well as three of Florida's more succulent residents: the shrimp, the stone crab, and the lobster.

Manatees and sea turtles graze on seagrass; dolphins, sharks, and rays patrol them in search of a snack. Elegantly housed conchs, tulips, and whelks can be found sliding over the beds as quickly as snails. Seagrass is one of the few species of flowering plants able to spend its complete life cycle underwater. It also acts as a filtering agent and stabilizes bottom sediments by trapping debris in the carpet of its bed.

"The health of the beloved coral reefs of the Florida Keys," said Jean-Michel Cousteau, president of the Ocean Futures Society, at a festival honoring seagrass, "depends upon the health of its seagrass habitat. Without the quiet beauty of seagrass meadows, the splendors of the coral reefs could not thrive. Like everything on our planet, the two are directly connected."

Above the Surface

Key Largo is the first island you encounter after leaving the mainland and is less than a two-hour drive from Miami International Airport—depending on the traffic. Key West, the southernmost destination, is a beautiful three- to four-hour drive from the airport. Only one road connects Key Largo to Key West, the 108-mile-long Overseas Highway, and those planning to snorkel in the Keys will have to spend at least a short time traversing it. However, with 43 bridges, a 34-foot lobster, Flipper's gravesite, and a refuge for miniature deer, the Overseas Highway has been designated one of America's Top Ten Scenic Drives by travel writers.

The majority of the highway is a thin stretch of asphalt with one lane traveling in each direction. Short green and white signs called mile markers are placed at the side of the road. Directions in the islands are given in terms of mile markers. Jewfish Creek Bridge,

The Florida Keys

1. Carysfort Reef
2. The Elbow
3. Jules' Undersea Lodge
4. John Pennekamp Coral
   Reef State Park
5. French Reef
6. Molasses Reef
7. Pickles Reef
8. Conch Reef
9. Founder's Park
10. Hens and Chickens
11. Davis Reef
12. Alligator Reef
13. Indian Key
14. The *San Pedro* Underwater
    Archeological Preserve
15. Coffins Patch Reef
16. Sombrero Beach
17. Delta Shoals
18. Sombrero Reef
19. Bahia Honda State Park
20. Looe Key
21. Newfound Harbor
22. Key West Marine Park
23. Sand Key
24. The Dry Docks
25. Cottrell Key
26. Marquesas Keys
27. Dry Tortugas

Marathon

Big Pine Key

19

21
20

Key West

25

22

26

27

23

Dry Tortugas

24

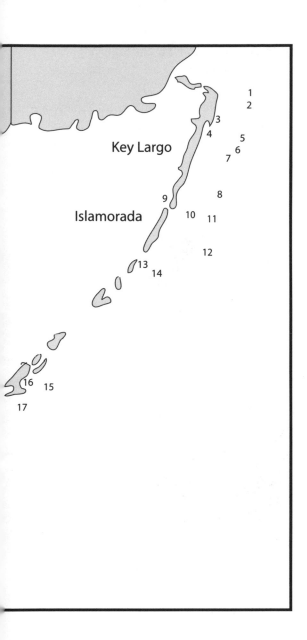

Key Largo

Islamorada

1
2
3
4
5
6
7
8
9
10 11
12
13 14
16 15
17

at Mile Marker 108 in Key Largo, is at one end of the highway. Mile Marker 0, at the other end, is just down the street from Hemingway's place in Key West.

Directions in the Keys are given not only in terms of mile markers but also in terms of Oceanside or Bayside, indicating the side of the road on which your destination is found. Traveling south, the Oceanside, or Atlantic Ocean side of the road, will always be on the left.

Mile Markers 108–95

Key Largo is the largest island in the chain and home to two communities, Key Largo and Tavernier. Key Largo, the city, wasn't always called Key Largo. It owes its name to the Humphrey Bogart movie, *Key Largo*. People still speculate as to whether Bogart ever actually set foot on the island during filming of the 1948 movie, which features the World Famous Caribbean Club at Mile Marker 105, Bayside. Back then, the town of Key Largo was actually called Rock Harbor. It was after the movie was released that 512 residents signed a petition, later passed by the rest of the townspeople, to have Rock Harbor officially renamed Key Largo.

Mile Markers 94–89

The town of Tavernier straddles two islands, Key Largo and the next key in the chain, Plantation Key. Tavernier Towne, a shopping center, is probably the closest thing to a town as there is in Tavernier. Found at Mile Marker 91, Tavernier Towne is home to the last major supermarket, the last movie theater, the last McDonald's, and the only hospital, Mariner's Hospital, this side of Marathon some 40 miles farther south.

The Wild Bird Center at Mile Marker 94, Bayside, is the local bird hospital and convalescent home. Whenever a pelican, heron, egret, or other feathered creature is found tangled in monofilament, pierced by a fishing hook, or otherwise injured, this is where it is taken for treatment.

The injured and the healing can be found in enclosed aviaries built on the grounds. While many of the birds are recuperating, some are permanent residents because of disabilities such as loss of sight or a wing. The Wild Bird Center operates on the generosity of cash donations, and at some point along the self-guided tour you will come upon a donation box requesting $5 per car.

On the naturally wooded lands, spiky-flowering bromeliads can be seen growing on overhead limbs and at least two species of orchids can be found. Part of the self-guided tour will take you through a tropical hammock. In these parts a hammock is considered a stand of indigenous trees, not a woven mat stretched between two trunks. The trees in this hammock, including strangler fig, gumbo-limbo, and poisonwood, are identified with small plaques. The poisonwood is so named because when leached, its sap burns like an acid.

Mile Markers 88–70

In Spanish, *Islamorada* means Purple Island. Islamorada, however, is not a single island but a collection of them. Locally referred to as a village of islands, Islamorada includes the keys Plantation, Windley, Upper and Lower Matecumbe, and Craig. The Chamber of Commerce claims that Islamorada is the sport fishing capital of the world, but for snorkelers, it is one of the premier snorkeling destinations in the state.

Snorkeling opportunities abound close to shore, but any snorkeler worth his salt will want to hitch a ride to the big corals offshore. Fortunately for those without a boat, it is hard to throw a coconut on these islands without hitting a charter outfit offering scheduled visits to the reefs. However, like Tavernier, the Islamorada charter boat industry tends to cater to scuba divers, and often the day's cargo will produce a mixed bag of both divers and snorkelers. While reef trips generally include two sites per trip, there are excursions where only one of the sites will be suitable for snorkelers, so it might be good to inquire where a prospective charter plans to go.

The biggest difference between one charter boat operation and another is the mile marker at which it is located. Bud and Mary's, at Mile Marker 80, will likely include Alligator Reef on their trip, while Holiday Isle's *Captain Scuba*, at the dock near Mile Marker 84, likes to visit a reef site called Hens and Chickens.

Local waters are world renowned for their warm and shallow nature and have aided in the pioneering advancement of underwater photography, marine biology, treasure salvage, diving, and snorkeling. History buffs will want to stop by the newly opened Florida Keys History of Diving Museum at Mile Marker 83, Bayside. The museum hosts enough gear, apparatus, and interactive displays to entertain anyone who has ever dreamed of being submersed. The museum is hard to miss, as two life-sized whale sharks have been painted into a mural on the museum's edifice.

Islamorada, however, is best known for its fishing. There is a reason the Chamber of Commerce bills this the "Sport Fishing Capital of the World." The species list on the fishing menu includes marlin (white and blue), swordfish, sailfish, tuna (black fin as well as the occasional yellow fin), wahoo, tarpon, permit, spotted sea trout, cobia, a list of snappers including yellowtail, mutton, red, cubera, vermilion, mahogany, and mangrove, bluefish, redfish, bonefish, barracuda, shark, mackerel (Spanish, cero, and king), snook, grouper, and dolphin (mahi-mahi in some regions of the world and dorado in others, but certainly not Flipper), to list a few. T-shirts sold at the Lor-e-lie, a bayside bar favored by backcountry fishing guides and sunset enthusiasts, might best sum up the Islamorada experience: "Islamorada, A Quaint Little Drinking Village with a Fishing Problem."

Islamorada is also home to the Big Lobster. A 34-foot anatomically correct sculpture, the Big Lobster resides at Treasure Village on the south end of Plantation Key. Stop the car for a once-in-a-lifetime photographic opportunity; everybody does. Based on a conservative yield of 200 pounds of tail meat, it would take about 80 friends and seven gallons of melted butter to devour the Big Lobster at a single dinner.

Islamorada's Big Lobster.

Mile Markers 69–35

The Middle Keys include Long Key, Conch Key, Duck Key, Grassy Key, Vaca Key, and Bahia Honda. Long Key was once called Rattlesnake Key, *Cayo Vibura* by the Spanish, not so much for its reptilian inhabitants but for the island's serpentine outline. Long Key State Park is located here. The park's scenery is breathtaking. Sixty Atlantic-front campsites, equipped with electricity and fresh water, are available. Campers should note that sites are available for no longer than 14-day stretches.

On Duck Key you can swim with dolphins at Hawk's Cay; on Grassy Key you can swim with them at the Dolphin Research Center, which is also the final resting place of the internationally recognized television star, Flipper. Two generations of her offspring have performed at the center.

Turtle Hospital Ambulance.

The city of Marathon is on Vaca Key. *Vaca* is Spanish for cow; it is rumored that once upon a time, manatees, also referred to as seacows, frequented the seagrass meadows surrounding the island. The Museums of Crane Point Hammock, in Marathon, display early Bahamian artifacts as well as those from pirates, shipwrecks, and both Calusa and Tequesta Indians. The Florida Keys Children's Museum offers a saltwater lagoon exhibit where children of all ages can reach out and touch living examples of the local ecology, including baby spiny lobster.

Marathon is also home to the Turtle Hospital. Whenever struggling turtles are found in the Keys' waters, Richie Moretti comes to their rescue. He runs the state-of-the-art facility responsible for the rehabilitation and release of over 800 turtles—so far.

The turtle hospital was once a hotel. The hotel's swimming pool is now a saltwater holding pen for recovering and permanent residents. Providing there has not been a turtle emergency, the hospital offers daily guided educational tours. Because tours are limited to 20 guests, reservations are recommended.

The leatherback, occasionally spotted in and around the reefs, is the largest living turtle in the world. A behemoth, the leatherback—named for its leathery shell—can grow to seven feet in length and weigh as much as 2,000 pounds. A total of five turtle species can be found in Florida waters including the leatherback, loggerhead, green, hawksbill, and Kemp's-Ridley.

Long-lived, turtles can grow to be over 70 years old, though most hatchlings fail to survive their first year, and only one in 1,000 hatchlings lives long enough to reach maturity. Sadly, not one of these reptile species boasts a healthy population, and of the five indigenous species, only the loggerhead is not classified as endangered; however, it is considered a threatened species. Turtle populations sizes are limited not only by lethal trash like plastic bags and cigarette butts and boats inadvertently striking them, but also by habitat loss due to human encroachment as their traditional nesting sites are being developed into condominiums.

Turtles become entangled in the ropes connecting lobster and crab traps to surface buoys. Monofilament, the scourge of the sea, gets ingested (hooks and all) by turtles or tangled around their flippers, which can, in cases, lead to amputation. Turtles love to eat shrimp and often mistake floating cigarette butts for them. They also confuse floating plastic bags for jellyfish, another favorite turtle snack. As if these threats were not enough, a mysterious herpes-like virus called *fibropapilloma* (Plate 2) has been attacking these turtles and causing tumors to grow over their eyes, on their flippers or underbelly, and sometimes internally.

Mile Markers 34–5

Big Pine Key, the second largest of the islands linked by the Overseas Highway, is home to the Blue Hole. This just might be your southernmost opportunity to view alligators in the wild. Named for the brilliant hue of its water, Blue Hole is the result of a former quarry pit dug by railroad workers during the construction of Henry Flagler's Overseas Railway. Key deer can also be seen sipping from the water's edges. Key deer are roughly the size of a Labrador

The infamous Perky's Bat Tower on Sugarloaf Key.

retriever and are considered the "toy" cousins of the white-tailed deer indigenous to most of North America, including Florida.

Big Pine Key is home to the National Key Deer Refuge. Deer roam freely about Big Pine as well as neighboring islands. Two of the better sighting sites are the northern end of Key Deer Boulevard on Big Pine and the east end of Watson Boulevard on nearby No Name Key. The deer can also been seen pillaging residential trash cans like common raccoons.

On Sugarloaf Key, behind the Sugarloaf Airport, at Mile Marker 17, Bayside, stands the Perky Bat Tower, a testament to shortsightedness. Perky, a would-be fishing camp entrepreneur, built the tower in 1929. In those days mosquitoes swarmed through the air like clouds. Lacking the advantage of modern-day pesticides, Perky planned to enlist bats to control the local mosquito population.

The idea was not his own but came from a Dr. Charles Campbell of San Antonio, Texas, who claimed to have scientifically designed the tower to attract and roost bats. Perky read about the tower in a magazine and invested in the project. He built the tower to specifications and spiced it with bat guano because to a bat, the smell of its own guano is the smell of home. However, when his mail-order bats arrived and he set the colony free at the foot of the tower, the bats flew up, up and away and were never seen again. Today Perky's bat tower is one of only three left standing in the world. The fishing camp, by the way, never came to fruition.

Unlike the Upper Keys, the big snorkeling action in the Lower Keys centers around one site, Looe Key, which is not an island but rather a large spur-and-groove reef formation. Finding passage to the reef is no harder than driving down the Overseas Highway. Charter outfits from Bahia Honda to Key West make the trip twice daily.

Mile Marker 0

In 1755 the sailing ship *Notre Dame de Deliverance* was engulfed by a hurricane off the coast of the Keys. When the weather cleared, 400 French shipwreck survivors were unfortunate enough to be met by a group of Calusa Indians. The Calusa killed the survivors and, having an apparent fondness for French cuisine, dined on them as well.

There are accounts that, one year later, a French Governor General stationed in the Caribbean heard about the massacre and sent 600 Spanish and French soldiers to retaliate. The soldiers found most of the Calusa tribe in Key West and promptly killed thousands of them. This might be one reason that Key West was once called *Cayo Hueso* or Bone Island. Say *Cayo Hueso* enough times or after enough rum and it is easy to see how Key West became an English bastardization of the Spanish *Cayo Hueso*.

Though just about every Key West story involves the mention of Duval Street, plenty of Key West quirkiness can be found off the island's official main drag. Along Duval's side streets, tropical gardens with extravagantly petaled orchids and the spiky red flower shoots of bromeliads grow fervently behind white picket fences. Wooden cottages are lavishly garnished with gingerbread mermaids, seashells, and flamingoes. Bananas and papaya grow wild. Chickens crow and quibble and can occasionally be spotted flying through the air like bowling balls.

Key West's residents have a history of spotting the noisome creatures and calling, "Fowl!" Not only do the birds kick, scratch, and dig up both landscaped and natural lands, but the bird-brained cocks have a reputation for mistaking streetlights, the moon, and lighted marquees for the rising sun. Key West's free-ranging fowl have long been covered under an umbrella of bird protection laws and city ordinances. In an effort to protect indigenous herons, egrets, spoonbills, and other feathered victims of the plume trade, the city of Key West declared itself a sanctuary for all of its feathered residents. Although the chickens are both adored and loathed, nothing ruffles residential feathers like they do.

Schooner Wharf is home to the Historic Key West Seaport. Many of Key West's snorkeling charters depart from Schooner Wharf, as do many fishing and general sightseeing charters. Schooner Wharf is also home port of the *Western Union*, a 130-foot double-masted sailing schooner modeled after the old wrecker ships used in the days of open piracy. The *Western Union* was the last tall ship built in Key West.

The nightly Sunset Celebration at Mallory Square is the quintessential Key West experience. Dogs jump through fire rings, Love 22 campaigns for president, fire breathers juggle, palm readers tell fortunes, and local artists selling their wares gather to create a bazaar atmosphere. When the sun begins to set, revelers raise their

The ubiquitous Key West chickens.

beverages to toast the sun, and when the last sliver of sun disappears, clapping can be heard.

Inhabiting the local waters are two creatures that are more talked about than others: the spiny lobster and the conch. Snorkelers visiting Key West, and in fact, all of the Keys, will hear continual references to conchs and lobsters. The more succulent of these is the Florida spiny lobster. The most obvious difference between a Florida spiny lobster and a Maine lobster is that the Florida variety possesses no claws; the majority of its meat is in the tail. Spiny lobsters are locally referred to as bugs and crayfish. Steamed, grilled, broiled, fried, frittered, bisqued, or stuffed with crabmeat, spiny lobster meat is rich and sweet.

By the light of day these lobsters like to hide in crevices. However, two long red spiny antennae often give away their location; they are just as likely to be spotted close to shore as they are out on a reef. To harvest them, a Florida saltwater fishing license is required as well as a crayfish endorsement. Hands, nets, and tickle sticks are the only legal ways to get them. Tickle sticks are used to coax these spiny crustaceans out from under crevices and ledges. Using any device capable of puncturing, penetrating, or crushing a lobster's exoskeleton is illegal.

When lobsters are harvested, the carapace must exceed three inches in total length for the lobster to be of legal size. The carapace is the body armor; it starts at the eye stalks and ends at the start of the tail. Measurements must be made underwater. Measuring devices can be purchased wherever lobster-hunting gear is sold. If you surface with an undersized specimen, a fine may be levied against you. Even with lobster of legal size, it is illegal to separate the crustacean from its tail until both have reached dry land. It is also illegal to take egg-bearing females. These females will have an egg mass clinging to the underside of the tail. Wiping an egg mass from a lobster's tail is both illegal and selfish.

Harvesting is legal during two seasons. The primary lobster season runs from August 6 through March 31. The Sport Season is a two-day affair that occurs on the last consecutive Wednesday and Thursday of July. Officially, the Sport Season begins at 12:01 Wednesday morning and ends at midnight on Thursday. There is no night diving for lobster in Monroe County during the Sport Season. Night is measured from one hour after the official sunset, to one hour before the official sunrise.

The bag limit is 12 lobsters per person per day for most of Florida. In Monroe County—the Keys—six per person per day is the limit. Any one boat is allowed to harvest 24 per day no matter how many licensed collectors are on board.

As for the conch, it is a sea snail. Conch, by the way, rhymes with honk and bonk, and locals can be quick to correct mispronunciations. Conch are quite large; their shells can grow to be as big as a football. Several species can be found in Florida waters including fighting conchs, helmet conchs, milk conchs, and horse conchs, the state shell of Florida. The pink-lipped queen conch is the most commercially viable species and garners most of the attention. As well as being the official symbol of the Conch Republic,

Conch shells, the symbol of the Conch Republic.

the shell of the queen is sold by the truckload at souvenir stands all along coastal Florida. Held against the ear, the shell will whisper the ocean's roar.

Early settlers of the Keys dined extensively on the conch's meat. Conch, specifically the queen, is not as prevalent now as it once was in Florida. Once upon a time a fisherman could fill his dinghy with live queen conch shells in a matter of hours. Commercial fisheries had nearly picked clean the wild populations of queens around the Keys by the early 1980s. Lawmakers officially banned both commercial and recreational harvesting in 1986. Once again, however, these magnificent mollusks are becoming a common sight in Florida waters.

How then, you may ask, can this be such a common dish found on restaurant menus? All conch served in Florida restaurants is either imported or farm raised. Key West's Florida Straits Conch Company is, among other things, a farm. Found on Schooner Wharf, the Conch Company has three functions: restaurant, farm, and educational facility. The restaurant features farm-raised queen conch; the farm has conch in various stages of maturation; the museum complex shows the special role this sea snail has played in the Keys' history.

In the Turks and Caicos Islands, the Caicos Conch Farm ships between 1,000 and 2,000 pounds of queen conch meat to Florida restaurants each week. Popular local fare, conch is served chowdered, fried, sautéed, steaked, sandwiched, and frittered, perhaps its most common preparation. Tossed with diced peppers, onion, tomato, key lime, and cilantro, it makes for a fabulous salad.

The Florida Keys are also affectionately known as the Conch Republic. The island nation was formed in 1982 after a traffic jam of stupendous magnitude plugged the 18-mile stretch of asphalt separating Key Largo from the mainland. The traffic jam made international headlines after the United States Army constructed a border checkpoint across the highway in front of the Last Chance Saloon at the southern edge of Florida City. The official explanation for the roadblock implicated the Keys as a major crossing passage for illegal aliens. Unofficially, the roadblock was suspected as a ploy to allow law enforcement agencies to search cars for drugs.

Because of the difficulty of getting out of the Keys, tourists stopped coming, and hotels, restaurants, and bars emptied. Key West Mayor Dennis Wardlow flew to Miami seeking an injunction against the U.S. Army in federal court. Failing to receive a judicial reprieve, Mayor Wardlow stood on the steps of the Miami courthouse and declared to the local paparazzi that the following day at noon the Keys would be seceding from the Union. During a ceremony held in Key West the following day the mayor declared the islands the Conch Republic, the World's First Fifth World Nation. The newly crowned country surrendered to the U.S. Navy the same day. Well adorned and slow moving, the conch is a fitting symbol for this tiny island nation.

REEF

The primary concern of REEF, the Reef Environmental Education Foundation, is the health and preservation of marine environments. The home office is in Key Largo, located on the median of the Overseas Highway around Mile Marker 97. Every July, REEF sponsors the Great Annual Fish Count. Begun in 1992 by a small group of recreational divers and marine biologists conducting 50 fish counts off the California coast, participants recorded, on handheld underwater slates, the numbers and species of fish observed through the course of their swim.

Today, snorkelers and divers from South America to Canada participate in the Great Annual Fish Count. As well as raising public awareness, fish counting gives researchers, marine resource managers, and policy-makers hard facts about marine environments.

In a statement issued by REEF,

Participation in REEF's survey program enhances a diver's ability to discern details about the marine environment. For divers that have no training as naturalists, areas begin to blend together and the attitude that it's just another coral reef or "one more kelp forest" prevails. The excitement of finding a rare fish can only be appreciated if one knows it's rare. By learning identification techniques and recording their fish observations, REEF surveyors become keen observers, true naturalists.

The REEF Web site, www.REEF.org, has information regarding training seminars teaching basic fish identification and recording skills. REEF fish-counting starter kits are also available and include underwater slates, paper, and fish ID cards in color.

1

Carysfort/South Carysfort Reef, Key Largo

Rating: Beginner to Advanced

Carsyfort is named for the H.M.S. *Carysfort*, a 28-gun frigate that ran aground here in 1770. A number of buoys mark this double-ledged spur-and-groove reef formation. The 112-foot lighthouse was built in 1848. The reef structures run basically in a straight line northwest and southeast of the lighthouse, and depths at this extensive reef structure range from 5 to 25 feet.

The reef is sometimes called the Fish Farm for the vast schools of goatfish, French grunts, pork fish, snappers, and parrotfish that school here (Plate 3). Stands of elkhorn corals rise toward the surface. Substantial beds of seagrass can be found near the first markers. To get a good look at colorful damselfish and sea anemones, swim in the shallow waters under and around the lighthouse.

Undaunted by the presence of the lighthouse, the captain of a 400-foot oil tanker called the *Maitland* ran aground on Carysfort in 1989. Making the worst of a bad situation, the captain shifted the boat into reverse and attempted to back off the reef—leaving 681 square meters of catastrophic damage behind. During the next few years, the prop scars grew an additional 40 percent, and by 1995, a crater-sized hole threatened to undermine the stability of the reef. Area biologist Harold Hudson, known in these parts as the Reef Doctor, led a group of divers to restructure the reef using concrete slabs.

This reef is an SPA, a Sanctuary Preservation Area. Carysfort is the largest SPA in the Keys. No collecting, fishing, or lobstering is allowed within the four yellow buoys marking the area.

GPS: N 25 12.20 / W 80 13.56
Directions: 5.6 nautical miles off the coast of Key Largo.
Hours of Operation: n/a

Visitor Information: n/a

Web site: n/a

Boat Ramp: John Pennekamp Coral Reef State Park, MM 102.5 O/S,
305.451.1202

2

The Elbow, Key Largo

Rating: Beginner to Advanced

Elbow Reef juts out toward the horizon like an elbow and is a fairly shallow spur-and-groove coral formation with depths ranging from 10 to 35 feet. Mooring buoys are available. Elbow Reef is an SPA. Multiple wrecks can be found here. The *City of Washington*, built in 1877, was a transport ship for troops during the Spanish-American War. The ship wrecked on July 10, 1917, and settled in 25 feet of water between mooring buoys 7 and 8. Artifacts include a ladder, porthole, and portions of the hull and deck.

The other discernible wreck is a Civil War wreck, a 752-foot steamer that sank in 1866. The ship's remains can be found in 10 to 15 feet of water between mooring buoys 5 and 6. There is not a great deal left of the ship, but you can still see the ribs. What is left has been coated with colorful sponges and corals.

Beautiful fish like angelfish and blue tangs will probably be loitering about somewhere near, and you should look for lobster hiding in the nooks and crannies of both reef and wreck structures. Their spiny red antennae generally give their position away. Don't stick your fingers into these spaces; both the spotted and the green moray eels might call them home.

GPS: N 25 08.25 / W 80 15.52
Directions: Approximately 5.5 miles southeast of Key Largo and
 marked by Lighted Marker 6.
Hours of Operation: n/a
Visitor Information: n/a
Web site: n/a
Boat Ramp: John Pennekamp Coral Reef State Park, MM 102.5 O/S,
 305.451.1202

3

Jules' Undersea Lodge, Key Largo

Rating: Beginner to Intermediate

The lagoon housing the "World's Only Underwater Hotel" is found at the end of Transylvania Avenue, perhaps the oddest name choice of any street in the whole of the island chain. This protected lagoon is as big as an Olympic-sized pool and the perfect destination when weather conditions are unfavorable out on the open water. The fee to snorkel here is $15 and includes rental of gear.

The hotel is not 20,000 leagues under the sea but a less daunting 30 feet below the surface. Concrete steps, accompanied by a hand railing, lead into the water. To reach the motel, you must swim 30 feet below the surface to the entrance. As for marine life sightings, they are always a game of chance, and the tide could bring in manatee, lobster, seahorse, butterflyfish, or angelfish.

Rates for the motel's occupancy range from a Mini Adventure of $125 for a three-hour stay to the Ultimate Romantic Getaway Package running over $1,200. This top-of-the-line stay includes fresh flowers, mood music, caviar, and a breakfast served by your very own mer-chef.

The motel used to be called La Chalupa and was designed in 1970 by an aquanaut named Ian Koblick. As a research lab, the La Chalupa Habitat homesteaded a 30-acre spread along the continental shelf off the coast of Puerto Rico. The submerged laboratory was used by the Marine Resources Development Foundation to show the value of managing marine resources onsite. In 1984, the foundation moved La Chalupa (anyone else getting hungry?) to Key Largo's John Pennekamp Coral Reef State Park, where it became known as the "Classroom in the Sea." In this incarnation, it became the setting where teachers and students who lived underwater studied the ocean.

The hotel, as it is seen today, opened for business in 1986 and lists hot showers, a telephone, air-conditioning, stereo music, VCRs, and a fully stocked galley on its list of amenities. While the living space is monitored 24 hours a day, there are no cameras in the bedrooms.

Address: 51 Shoreland Drive, Key Largo.

Directions: Turn left on Transylvania Avenue near Mile Marker 103, Oceanside.

Hours of Operation: 8:00 a.m. to 4:00 p.m., seven days a week.

Visitor Information: 305.451.2353

Web site: www.jul.com

Boat Ramp: Unnecessary

4

John Pennekamp Coral Reef State Park, Key Largo

Rating: Beginner to Advanced

John Pennekamp park is in a natural mangrove setting with camping facilities, nature trails, beaches, kayak and boat rentals, picnicking, canoeing, fishing, sunning, and snorkeling. The Spanish cannons decorating the park are artifacts salvaged from galleons that wrecked offshore. The majority of the park is located underwater; a number of reef sites are encompassed. Park concessionaires provide ample passage via chartered snorkeling trips, boat rentals, and glass-bottom boat tours.

Snorkeling off the beach is excellent for young snorkelers or those looking for a casual spot to get acclimated to their equipment. Keep in mind that these are heavily trafficked areas and they might not prove as prolific—in terms of biodiversity—as other seagrass environments. They do, however, have their merit.

The Christ of the Abyss (GPS: N 25 06.91 / W 80 18.20), a nine-foot bronze statue that can be found at the Key Largo Dry Rocks, might be the most visited snorkeling site in the Sunshine State. This is an SPA. Duplicated from a sister statue found off the coast of Genoa, Italy, this Christ of the Abyss stands in 20 feet of water between mooring buoys 4 and 5. If you are snorkeling from a charter boat, this will generally be one of the two sites visited in the Pennekamp area.

Grecian Rocks (GPS: N 25 07.59 / W 80 17.91) is another site ideal for snorkelers of all comfort levels. This is an SPA. While depths reach as much as 35 feet, at low tide some parts of this site lie exposed to the sun. Look for lobsters in the cracks and crevices as well as eels and crabs. Colorful tropicals, including damselfish and angelfish, will stick close to the rocks as well.

Address: Mile Marker 102.5, Oceanside, Key Largo.
Directions: Mile Marker 102.5, Oceanside.
Hours of Operation: 8:00 a.m. to sunset, 365 days a year.
Visitor Information: 305.451.1202
Web site: www.floridastateparks.org/pennekamp/
Boat Ramp: Yes

5

French Reef, Key Largo

Rating: Beginner to Advanced

French Reef has spur-and-groove reef formations, and depths range from 15 to 40 feet. Mooring buoys can be found at this site. Currents can be strong, so it might be best to call a Key Largo area dive shop to check on existing current conditions before venturing out. French Reef is best known for its caves and hollowed-out coral structures. French Reef is an SPA.

Large stands of elkhorn corals and sponges can be found here. Schools of minnowy fish will huddle in the caves. If you have the opportunity, take a deep breath, dive down, and let a school of them engulf you. Larger fish like grouper and mutton snapper will also seek refuge beneath ledges and in caves. This is a favorite resting spot of loggerhead turtles and nurse sharks.

If you have the lungs for it, just west of the mooring buoy marked F3, you will find a large, doughnut-like structure that you can swim through. Should you take a deep breath and dive down, remember not to touch the sides. Near the buoy marked F7 is an old Spanish anchor.

GPS: N 25 02.20 / W 80 20.63
Directions: North of Molasses Reef, French Reef is about 6 miles
     southeast of Key Largo.
Hours of Operation: n/a
Visitor Information: n/a
Web site: n/a
Boat Ramp: John Pennekamp Coral Reef State Park, MM 102.5 O/S,
     305.451.1202

6

Molasses Reef, Tavernier

Rating: Beginner to Advanced

Molasses Reef is a tremendous example of a spur-and-groove reef system. The reef was named for a molasses barge that wrecked and sank here. Multiple mooring buoys mark this site and for good reason—Molasses Reef is thought to be the most frequently visited reef in the Upper Keys; it is also considered one of the most frequented reefs in the world. The whole family can find some part of this reef site to float over comfortably, as depths range from 5 to 40 feet. Should you have your own boat, be advised that the reef is shallowest near Lighted Marker 10. The mooring buoys marked from M1 to M25 are the best places to start. Molasses Reef is an SPA.

Molasses Reef is known for large schools of fish skirting between and around its great many nooks, crannies, gaps, and ledges. Turtles cruise by from time to time, attracted by healthy populations of the sponges on which they feed. Jewfish, the former and politically incorrect name for the Goliath grouper, can also be occasionally spotted in the shadows of this reef.

An eight-foot Spanish anchor can be found here; it is thought to have been left behind by the gale of 1733, which grounded over 20 treasure ships, among other vessels. To find the anchor, look near the buoy marked 3. Queen conch and starfish (Plate 4) are sometimes in the seagrass growing near Marker 10. This site is also home to a large moray eel reportedly longer than six feet in length. Should you happen to view this specimen swimming out in the open, do not tug on its tail. It could very well bite you.

In 1984, the *Wellwood*, a 400-foot freighter carrying chicken feed, grounded on Molasses Reef near the mooring buoys marked M11 and M12. More than 20 years later the damage is still evident.

Take a moment to think about the hull of a ship longer than a football field lodged here.

Northeast of Lighted Marker 10 is a fourth buoy marking Sand Island. Sand Island is just shallow enough to snorkel over. The surrounding corals are in 15 to 25 feet of water. Sand Island is not considered an SPA. While no spearfishing is allowed, lobster can be taken during the season, which runs from August 6 through March 31.

GPS: N 25 01.00 / W 80 22.53

Directions: Found adjacent to a 45-foot steel tower designated
    Lighted Marker 10.

Hours of Operation: n/a

Visitor Information: n/a

Web site: n/a

Boat Ramp: Harry Harris Park, MM 92.5 O/S

7

Pickles Reef, Tavernier

Rating: Beginner to Advanced

This is not as frequented a reef as some of the others in the area, and both the seagrass and the shallow corals growing in 15 to 25 feet of water are perfect for snorkelers to explore. While a number of mooring buoys mark the area, the two buoys farthest south are closest to the reef. Pickles Reef is an SPA.

Pickles Reef is named for a Civil War–era wreck. The ship was carrying, among other items, dry cement stored in pickle barrels. During the wreck the pickle barrels came to rest on the bottom. Subsequently, the seawater set the barrels' contents. As the wood deteriorated, the barrel shaped structures became exposed. To find the barrels, moor at the buoy farthest north; the wreck lies in about 16 feet of water.

This site has a fairly large area of shallow seagrass beds that are ideal environments for spotting starfish and conch. Pickles Reef is also said to have one of the healthiest gardens of pillar corals in the whole of the barrier reef chain. There is another wreck at this site, a shrimp boat, though there is not much to see and the wreck can prove difficult to find. To discover what little evidence remains of this wreck, patrol the shallower waters between the pillar corals and the rubble fields.

GPS: N 24 59.23 / W 80 24.88
Directions: Pickles Reef is about 2 miles southwest of Molasses
  Reef.
Hours of Operation: n/a
Visitor Information: n/a
Web site: n/a
Boat Ramp: Harry Harris Park, MM 92.5 O/S

8

Conch Reef, Tavernier

Rating: Intermediate to Advanced

Conch Reef is made up of eight distinct patch reefs growing in depths from 12 to 30 feet. Mooring buoys mark the site, and for the best snorkeling, use one of the three buoys north of Marker 12. Conch Reef is an SPA.

Queen conchs have been rare finds in these waters for longer than most locals can remember. However, small populations of queen conch are beginning to accumulate off the coast of the Keys. Conch Reef is one site where it is becoming more common to spy them, though not necessarily crawling over the corals. Spend at least a little time looking in the seagrass shallows north of the patch reefs. Should you be lucky enough to spot a queen conch, remember that they are a protected species and cannot, under any circumstance, be collected.

Remains of the Spanish ship, *El Infante*, lost in the hurricane of 1733, are still seen from time to time. The treasures from this wreck were taken decades ago, but then again, you never know what might still be out there. Wave your hand over the sandy bottom near the reef structures in hopes of uncovering a doubloon— stranger things have happened!

Aquarius, an underwater laboratory, is located beneath an area marked by four excessively large yellow buoys. This section of the reef is intended for research only, and because of its depth, it is completely unsuited for snorkeling. Should curiosity get the better of you, do not be surprised if your overt act garners unwanted attention from local authorities.

GPS: N 24 56.55 / W 80 28.43
Directions: Less than 4 nautical miles south of Tavernier Key near Marker 12.

Hours of Operation: n/a
Visitor Information: n/a
Web site: n/a
Boat Ramp: Harry Harris Park, 92.5 O/S

9

Hens and Chickens, Islamorada

Rating: Beginner to Advanced

A hen-and-chickens, florally speaking, is a collection of succulents growing in runners or clusters. The reef Hens and Chickens is a patch reef with one major cluster of corals, the Hen, and several budding patch reefs, or Chickens, surrounding it. Mooring buoys are available. Depths range from 5 to 20 feet. Hens and Chickens is an SPA. Because of its proximity to shore, the reef can be affected by tidal surge; for the best visibility, visit during slack tide.

Many large coral heads—make that coral boulders—can be found. Some of them are carpeted with brain coral the color of lime sherbet and some are garnished with purple sea rods. Sea rods look a little like peacock feathers as they sway in the currents. Swim over the different coral patches and look for parrotfish, angelfish, surgeonfish, spadefish, and yellowtail snapper. Because the reef is reasonably close to shore, it is not uncommon to spot squadrons of snook patrolling the area in search of a quick snack.

The Brick Barge is an old iron ship that was torpedoed on Hens and Chickens during World War II. Like any wreck, the ship has become heavily encrusted with corals, sponges, and other marine structures. What is left of the ship, which isn't much, can be found on the north side of the reef in 20 to 30 feet of water.

Hens and Chickens is also in the vicinity of the Sandbar. On holiday weekends and summer afternoons, the Sandbar is where local boaters anchor down, splash around, and pop the tab on a cold one. The Sandbar is practically a stone's throw from the Overseas Highway and borders both sides of Whale Harbor Channel. If you have ever wondered what boater gridlock looks like, all you have to do is witness the madness of the Sandbar on a sunny holiday weekend.

GPS: N 24 55.86 / W 80 32.95

Directions: Marked by the 35-foot tower, Marker 40, Hens and Chickens grows in the middle of Hawks Channel, approximately 2 nautical miles east-southeast of Snake Creek. Snake Creek is the dividing body of water separating Plantation Key from Windley Key.

Hours of Operation: n/a

Visitor Information: n/a

Web site: n/a

Boat Ramp: Harry Harris Park, 92.5 O/S

10

Davis Reef, Islamorada

Rating: Intermediate to Advanced

Mooring buoys are available at this outer reef; it grows in 20 to 30 feet of water. The reef line runs in basically a straight line—which makes it easy to follow. Davis is not as heavily used as some of the other local reefs and is considered relatively healthy. It is also an SPA.

While snorkeling over the reef, you will usually see fish like yellowtail snapper, grunts, parrotfish, and angelfish. The real action, however, will be just out of view of those snorkelers content with swimming at the surface. The ledges undercutting the bottom of the reef form mini-caves where schools of colorful fish can be seen. This is also a favorite resting spot for turtles and nurse sharks.

Davis Reef might be best known for a bronze statue called the Happy Buddha. This statue, about the size of a basketball, sits serenely in the sand at the southern end of the reef. Rubbing the Buddha's belly is said to bring good luck, and the act comes highly recommended. Snorkelers who have rubbed the Buddha's belly have reported finding soulmates, landing dream jobs, and locating pots of gold at the ends of rainbows.

GPS: N 24 55.32 / W 80 30.36
Directions: 4 miles south of Plantation Key near Marker 14.
Hours of Operation: n/a
Visitor Information: n/a
Web site: n/a
Boat Ramp: Harry Harris Park, MM 92.5 O/S

11

Founder's Park, Islamorada

Rating: Beginner to Advanced

Founder's Park is perfect for families looking for a low-key beach-side getaway. Unless you are an Islamorada resident, admission to the park is $10 per vehicle. The small crescent-shaped beach is strewn with coconut palms and surrounded by a playground, dog park, and the Plantation Yacht Club. The swimming area is roped off. When snorkeling outside the roped-off swimming area,

Founder's Park, Plantation Key.

you are required to use dive flags; these can be rented from the concession shack on the beach. Snacks, sodas, beach chairs, and catamarans are also available.

Snorkeling within the roped-off swimming area, children will get a kick out of seeing small fish darting through clumps of sea-grass and the occasional crab scurrying across the bottom. If you venture out from the confines of the rope—dive flag in tow—you will see rock jetties extending from both the north and south ends of the park; these are generally packed with small barracuda, ser-geant majors, grunts, and snappers. Angelfish and butterflyfish are not everyday visitors but can sometimes be spotted. Tropically scaled parrotfish also fly through on occasion. While lobsters are generally prevalent, collecting them is not allowed this close to shore.

A hard-bottom coral community can be found about 20 yards out from the southern rock jetties. This is no coral reef, but a sig-nificant number of corals can be seen including at least one star coral head the size of a boulder. Because of their shallow nature, these inshore hard-bottom coral communities are particularly vul-nerable to human contact. The water is shallow enough that you can stand up here, and because of that, it is especially important to be aware of your body and not kick or stand on the corals.

If you don't want to get wet, take a stroll along the docks of the marina next door, where you can see snappers, grunts, parrotfish, and the occasional lobster. For lobster-spotting, look along the ma-rina wall for the tips of spiny red antennas sticking out.

Address: 86500 Overseas Highway, Plantation Key.
Directions: Mile Marker 86.5, Bayside.
Hours of Operation: 8:00 a.m. to sunset.
Visitor Information: 305.853.1685
Web site: n/a
Boat Ramp: Unnecessary

12

Alligator Reef, Islamorada

Rating: Beginner to Advanced

Alligator Reef is named for the U.S.S. *Alligator*, a 12-cannon schooner employed to combat piracy that grounded here in 1822. To keep pirates from pillaging the ship, what was not removed by the captain and crew was set afire. Alligator Reef is one of the easiest reefs to find because it is marked by a massive lighthouse. Alligator Light is 136-feet tall and visible from the Overseas Highway from Snake Creek Bridge to Lower Matecumbe Key. Mooring buoys mark Alligator Reef and depths range from 8 to 50 feet. An extensive reef system, this is considered one of the largest reefs in the chain. Alligator Reef is an SPA.

The reef is seemingly carpeted in purple seafans and purple sea rods. Swimming near the light, you will see surgeonfish, parrotfish, and a collection of snapper species. If large barracuda unnerve you, do not swim under the lighthouse; a number of the large torpedoesque fish regularly hang out there. The submerged structures supporting the light are great places to find clusters of small corals and sponges as well as worms, crabs, and other marine invertebrates.

Remnants of the U.S.S. *Alligator* are hard to spot but still visible. Most of the evidentiary artifacts come in the form of the ship's ballast stones. What remains of the ship can be found in about 10 feet of water. The mooring buoy located closest to the light marks the wreck site.

On the other end of the telescopic lens, 3.5 miles northwest of Alligator Reef, on the southern tip of Upper Matecumbe Key, is Lazy Days Restaurant. The restaurant has a brilliant Atlantic view, and Chef Lupe serves up some of the best food in all of the islands—ask any local. Try the Lazy Days Conch appetizer—shredded conch,

Alligator Light
marking
Alligator Reef.

formed into a patty, covered with Japanese breadcrumbs, cooked on a flat-top grill, and sprinkled with scallions, diced tomatoes, Parmesan cheese, and key lime butter. Delicious.

GPS: N 24 51.07 / W 80 37.21
Directions: 3.5 miles southeast of Upper Matecumbe Key.
Hours of Operation: n/a
Visitor Information: n/a
Web site: n/a
Boat Ramp: Indian Key Fill, MM 79, B/S

13

Indian Key State Historical Site, Islamorada

Rating: Beginner to Advanced

Indian Key is an 11-acre island in the Atlantic Ocean that isn't much more than a coconut's throw from the road. Once upon a time a thriving community and hotel were found on the island, which is accessible only by boat or kayak. Birds and mosquitoes are the only inhabitants now. There are no bathroom facilities, grills, tables, or concessions on the island, so you must pack in everything you need and pack out everything you use. The island is, however, a great spot for a picnic. This is Florida, so bring bug repellent. Indian Key is an SPA.

The best snorkeling is on the backside of the island. Enter the water from the island or directly from your kayak. Stunning examples of individual corals are visible in quite shallow waters; in some cases the water is knee-deep. These corals are particularly vulnerable to snorkelers so be extra careful not to harm them with

Indian Key, only a 20-minute kayak from Robbie's Marina.

your touch or kick. The environment is rich with beds of seagrass, sponges, and both hard and soft corals. The water surrounding the island ranges from too shallow to snorkel to four or five feet deep.

While kayaking out to the island, watch the seagrass beds for reddish-orange cushion starfish and purple sea urchins. Sponges of all shapes can be seen as well as purple and yellow tropicals the size of a fingernail. Look for the spiny red antennae of lobster sticking out from under the corals and sponges.

In 1831, Indian Key was home to 100 residents and owned by a man named Jacob Housman. The road system from the former colony is still intact and placards documenting the island's history have been placed around the island. Housman was a bit of a nefarious fellow and ran his own wrecking company from the island.

For those wondering what the difference between wrecking and piracy is, this is the skinny: when pirating, the captain takes everything found aboard a floundering vessel and splits a percentage with his crew. Wreckers did the same thing, only they ponied up 10 percent of the take to the government. On August 7, 1840, as many as 100 Calusa Indians attacked the island. Most of the inhabitants escaped alive.

To reach the island, you can rent kayaks from Florida Keys Kayak and Ski at Robbie's Marina located at Mile Marker 77.5. It takes only 25 minutes to paddle to the island from the marina. The Hungry Tarpon, the restaurant at the marina, is a great local spot for breakfast or lunch. This is also where you can feed the tarpon. Hordes of these massive silver fish, some as big as Superman, cruise beneath the old wood dock. One dollar provides access to the dock and, for three dollars more, the marina's staff will hand over a small blue bucket of bait with which you can feed the tarpon.

Address: 77500 Overseas Highway, Lower Matecumbe Key.
Directions: Mile Marker 77.5, Bayside.
Hours of Operation: 8:00 a.m. to sunset, 365 days a year.
Visitor Information: 305.664.2540
Web site: www.floridastateparks.org/indiankey/
Boat Ramp: Indian Key Fill, MM 79, B/S

14

The *San Pedro* Underwater Archaeological Preserve and State Park, Islamorada

Rating: Intermediate to Advanced

While this wreck is technically close enough to shore to paddle a kayak to, one and one-quarter miles south of Indian Key, kayaking is recommended only for those with experience. Should you make the trip, taking a GPS unit is recommended. Sitting in a kayak keeps you pretty low to the horizon and the mooring buoys marking the site are hard to spot until you get right on top of them. This is an SPA.

The sailing ship *San Pedro* was part of a Spanish treasure fleet lost to a hurricane in 1733. The wreck lies in 18 feet of water and is part of the State of Florida Underwater Archaeological Preserve. No collecting is allowed, including lobstering, crabbing, and spearfishing. Because of its proximity to shore, this shallow wreck is affected by the tidal flow. For best results, catch the *San Pedro* on the slack tide when the current has come to a standstill.

When the tide is right and the sun is bright, the cannons and ballast piles below can be clearly seen from the surface. There is not much else left from the wreck. While schools of snapper and grunts will shimmer by in the open water, you will also be able to see smaller tropicals, including damselfish and wrasses, skirting the ballast piles and coral structures.

When a snorkeler sees the remnants of a shipwreck in the water, 99.9 percent of the time the artifacts will have been planted naturally. The *San Pedro* site is a rare exception. The cannons at this site are authentic, but the original cannons of the ship disappeared a long time ago; the ones visible here have been planted by the state to enhance the wreck site.

GPS: N 24 51.802 / W 80 40.795
Directions: 1.25 nautical miles south of Indian Key.
Hours of Operation: n/a
Visitor Information: n/a
Web site: n/a
Boat Ramp: Indian Key Fill, MM 79, B/S

15

Coffins Patch Reef, Key Colony Beach

Rating: Beginner to Advanced

Coffins Patch is rumored to have been named after a ship that ran aground here carrying a load of empty coffins. The reef is actually a collection of small oval patch reefs growing in relatively shallow water. Depths range from 10 to 25 feet. The *Ignacio*, another Spanish galleon of the 1733 Treasure Fleet destroyed by a hurricane, wrecked here—though evidence of this is no longer clearly visible. The reef system is an SPA, so no harvesting or fishing is allowed. While there are big schools of fish, plenty of lobster, and a great many healthy coral gardens, there are no mooring buoys. When anchoring, take care not to drop your anchor atop any of the corals.

As you swim over the various patch reefs you will see a tremendous variety of fish species, along with pillar and elkhorn corals. Brush up on your fish identification skills or take a laminated fish ID chart with you. Along with the usual mix of damselfish and angelfish, frequent visitors are Nassau groupers, eagle rays, turtles, and hogfish.

GPS: N 24 41.10 / W 80 57.85
Directions: 4 miles southeast of Key Colony Beach.
Hours of Operation: n/a
Visitor Information: n/a
Web site: n/a
Boat Ramp: Marathon, MM 54, B/S

16

Sombrero Beach, Marathon

Rating: Beginner to Intermediate

There are few beaches lining the Keys, and fewer still of this quality. Sombrero is a public beach, and there is no fee to gain access to the property. Amenities include grills, showers, restrooms, a volleyball area, and a playground. This is a fairly manicured beach and is handicap accessible. Diver Down flags are unnecessary in the roped-off swimming area. This is a great site for the family to enjoy.

Experienced snorkelers may not find the environment exciting, but younger snorkelers will have a ball exploring the seagrass beds. There is no telling what you might see. Seagrass beds act as a nursery for many of the species found on the reefs offshore and are frequently home to starfish, lobster, crabs, and snails of all shapes and sizes.

Turtle season is from April to October, and it is not uncommon to find turtle nests on the beach throughout these months. Nests will be clearly marked, and it is important to respect the borders identified. Mother sea turtles go through a lot of work lugging their bodies over the beach and digging out a nest where as many as 100 golf-ball-sized eggs are laid.

Address: MM 50, Oceanside
Directions: Traveling south on the Overseas Highway, take a left on Sombrero Boulevard.
Hours of Operation: 7:00 a.m. to dusk.
Visitor Information: n/a
Web site: n/a
Boat Ramp: Unnecessary

17

Delta Shoals, Marathon

Rating: Beginner to Advanced

Delta Shoals is approximately one-half-mile long. This site is unmarked and provides no mooring buoys. When anchoring, look for a sandy place on the bottom to secure the boat. The corals grow in spur-and-groove formations in 10 to 25 feet of water.

Multiple shipwrecks can be found here including the Delta Shoals Barge and the Ivory Coast Wreck, a slave ship that sank in 1853. Little is left of either wreck, though once upon a time, divers found six-foot-long ivory elephant tusks here.

Lobster can be found under coral ledges as well as under the heads of brain and star corals. Because this is not a protected site, succulent stone crabs and spiny lobsters are fair game, and spearfishing is also allowed.

Another wreck found close to the shoal is thought to be the *North America*, a 130-foot, three-masted schooner lost on November 25, 1842, in 14 feet of water. The ship is just north of the shoal one mile east of Sombrero Light. GPS: N 24 38.270 / W 81 05.605. The *North America* was originally constructed in Bath, Maine, in 1833.

GPS: N 24 37.91 / W 81 05.43
Directions: 1 mile east of Sombrero Light.
Hours of Operation: n/a
Visitor Information: n/a
Web site: n/a
Boat Ramp: 7-Mile Bridge, MM 40 B/S

18

Sombrero Reef, Marathon

Rating: Beginner to Advanced

This is another snorkeling destination that is remarkably easy to find as it is marked by a 142-foot lighthouse, the tallest in the Keys, that is clearly visible from the 7-Mile Bridge. Sombrero is a large reef structure with spur-and-groove reef formations. Mooring buoys mark the site and depths range from 2 to 25 feet. This is an SPA.

As Sombrero Reef is the only major reef in the area, it can get a little crowded here, especially on the weekends. The seagrass beds and rubble field west of the light are especially suited for younger snorkelers venturing out on their own. On the reef, all the major hard corals can be found including star, sheet, brain, elkhorn, and staghorn. The reef is pocked with soft corals, purple fans, and plumes that sway elegantly with the current (Plate 5). Seahorses can sometimes be found with their tails wrapped around the stalks of soft corals. This is not only true for Sombrero Reef; seahorses can be found on every reef from Key Biscayne to the Dry Tortugas—though sighting one of them is fairly uncommon.

This reef has a number of cleaning stations, places where larger fish like barracuda and grouper stop to have smaller fish like gobies pick them clean of parasites. Cleaning stations are the fish version of a car wash. Fish wait in line to get cleaned, and as soon as one fish swims away from the station, another will park itself.

GPS: N 24 37.62 / W 81 06.36
Directions: 4.5 miles south of Marathon.
Hours of Operation: n/a
Visitor Information: n/a
Web site: n/a
Boat Ramp: 7-Mile Bridge, MM 40 B/S

19

Bahia Honda State Park, Bahia Honda

Rating: Beginner to Advanced

Bahia Honda is home to one of the deepest natural channels in the island chain, which is how it got its name. *Bahia Honda* is Spanish for deep channel. Like all state parks, entrance requires a small fee. The park's concessions are open until 5 p.m. The amenities at Bahia Honda include picnicking, kayak rentals, boat slips, restrooms, hot showers, camping, snorkeling equipment, and a gift shop/snack bar serving pizza and sandwiches.

Bahia Honda, the best beach snorkel in Florida.

Snorkeling from shore can be done on both the bay and ocean sides of the park. Colorful sponges, small corals, lobsters, colorful tropicals, and a host of other reef creatures are regularly spotted in the shallows off the beaches. Dive flags are required. The best snorkeling is done on the Atlantic Ocean side at the south end of the park.

The park's dive shop charters its boat to Looe Key at 8:30 a.m. and 12:00 p.m. daily, weather conditions permitting. This far down in the Keys, Looe Key, 20 miles south of Sombrero Reef, is the primary offshore snorkeling destination. During summer months a third trip is offered and departs from the park around 3:00 p.m.

Bahia Honda was voted America's Best Beach in Dr. Beach's 1992 survey. Beaches are somewhat hard to come by in the Keys, but this one is spectacular. With both bayside and oceanside beaches, this is a fantastic spot to unpack the family for a day or week.

Address: Mile Marker 37.
Directions: 12 miles south of Marathon.
Hours of Operation: 8:00 a.m. to sunset, 365 days a year.
Visitor Information: 305.872.2353
Web site: www.floridastateparks.org/bahiahonda/
Boat Ramp: Yes

20

Looe Key, Ramrod Key

Rating: Beginner to Advanced

Looe Key is not actually a key but a series of spur-and-groove reef structures. This is the top snorkeling site in the Lower Keys. Mooring buoys mark the reef where depths range from 5 to 40 feet. The Looe Key National Marine Sanctuary extends 5.3 miles around the reef system, which represents over 7,000 years of reef growth. Looe Key is an SPA.

Like many of the local reefs, Looe Key was named for a ship that wrecked here. The British warship, the H.M.S. *Looe*, hit the reef in 1744 while towing a captured French ship. The *Looe* sank in 25 feet of water about 200 yards east of the marker. Scant evidence remains of the ship, but snorkelers can still see the ship's ballast stones.

Like Marathon's Sombrero Reef, Looe Key is the only major reef in the area, which makes it the most popular place to snorkel in the Lower Keys. The reef can be jammed with boats and bodies.

Looe Key is also the site of the annual Underwater Music Festival held every July for the past 20 years. Sponsored by the Lower Keys Chamber of Commerce, this is the one time of year snorkelers can swim over the reefs while jazz, Caribbean rhythms, and Jimmy Buffett songs are broadcast through underwater speakers.

GPS: N 24 33.19 / W 81 24.77
Directions: Approximately 5.5 miles south of Ramrod Key.
Hours of Operation: n/a
Visitor Information: n/a
Web site: n/a
Boat Ramp: Cudjoe Key, MM 20 B/S

21

Newfound Harbor Patch Reefs, Newfound Harbor

Rating: Beginner to Advanced

This is a very shallow patch reef with depths of less than 10 feet. Mooring buoys mark the site. The Newfound Harbor area was also the setting for the 1962 movie *PT 109*, a film based on the war adventures of President John F. Kennedy. Newfound Harbor is an SPA.

Because of the reef's shallow nature, divers generally do not visit it. For the same reason, this site is especially suited for children and snorkelers uncomfortable in deeper waters. These patch reefs have a good deal of both hard and soft corals as well as a host of colorful tropicals like angelfish and parrotfish. Additionally, the occasional dolphin has been known to visit.

The two main patch reefs are protected, but other areas outside the yellow marking buoys are open to those who want to catch lobster or spear fish. Newfound Harbor is also home to the Newfound Harbor Marine Institute. Formed in 1966, this educational facility is for students from fourth grade through college and for educators who want to hone their marine ecology skills.

GPS: N 24 36.80 / W 81 23.30
Directions: 0.5 miles northeast of Newfound Harbor.
Hours of Operation: n/a
Visitor Information: n/a
Web site: n/a
Boat Ramp: Cudjoe Key, MM 20 B/S

22

Key West Marine Park, Key West

Rating: Beginner to Advanced

Even though the reefs lie a few miles offshore, snorkelers should not assume there is nothing to see right off the beach—even in Key West. A wonderful hard-bottom coral community including both hard and soft corals grows within shuffling distance from shore. In the hound-you-for-every-buck atmosphere that Key West can sometimes present, the park refreshingly requires no guides, no reservations, and no admittance fee.

Southernmost Point, where everyone stops for a picture.

The best snorkeling can be found off of Reynolds Avenue. There are occasional conchs, urchins, and sea stars in the seagrass beds. Orange sponges and yellow butterflyfish can be seen as well as the occasional spotted eagle ray, spiny lobster, nurse shark, and tropically scaled parrotfish. This is a protected area, and snorkelers are welcome to look but not to touch. Because boats are not allowed in the area, dive flags are not required.

Reef Relief is responsible for the Key West Marine Park. Reef Relief is a nonprofit membership organization dedicated to preserving and protecting living coral reef ecosystems through local, regional, and global efforts. Their Key West office is located near the end of Lazy Way Lane at historic Schooner Wharf.

The environmental center and store, at 201 William Street, is an educational facility free of charge and open to the public. It offers a short movie presentation on corals as well as a coral reef diorama, photographs, displays, and children's activities regarding reefs, turtles, dolphins, and sharks. This is an ideal educational resource for children of all ages.

Address: From the Atlantic Ocean end of Duval Street to the White Street Pier.

Directions: Each of the park's four entry points are accessible by foot: South Beach at Duval Street, Dog Beach at the end of Vernon Street, Mary and John Spottswood Waterfront Park at the foot of Seminole Street, and Higgs Beach from Reynolds Street to White Street.

Hours of Operation: Sunrise to sunset daily.

Visitor Information: n/a

Web site: www.reefrelief.org/MarinePark/

Boat Ramp: Unnecessary

23

Sand Key, Key West

Rating: Beginner to Advanced

Sand Key is exposed only at low tide. Seeing Sand Key, it can be hard to imagine that for 100 years lighthouse keepers made this scratch of land home. Mooring buoys mark the site along with a 109-foot red, iron lighthouse. Depths range from dry land to 60 feet deep. This is an SPA.

Fire corals are prevalent at the site. Remember that these corals often branch, and their tips will be whitish. Snorkelers can still come across pieces of the original brick lighthouse erected in 1827. That lighthouse, along with its occupants, was destroyed in a hurricane on October 11, 1846.

For those on charter boats from Key West, Sand Key will likely be on the agenda as this is a major stomping ground for local boats. High visitation has taken its toll on the corals. The lighthouse can be seen for miles, and on clear days, Key West can be seen from atop the tower.

Rock Key, one mile east of Sand Key, is completely submerged and is the site of two old wrecks scattered in 15 feet or so of water. While the coral heads will be self-evident, cannon balls, brass spikes, and Spanish tiles are still occasionally found by snorkelers. A shallow reef, its depths range from 5 to 35 feet. Mooring buoys mark the site. Rock Key is an SPA.

GPS (Rock Key): N 24 26.94/ W 81 51.38
GPS (Sand Key): N 24 27.57/ W 81 52.31
Directions: 7 miles southwest of Key West.
Hours of Operation: n/a
Visitor Information: n/a
Web site: n/a
Boat Ramp: Key West Garrison Bight Marina, 1801 N. Roosevelt
    Blvd., 305.292.8167

24

The Dry Docks, Key West

Rating: Beginner to Advanced

There are two sets of Dry Docks: Eastern and Western. The Eastern Dry Docks lie one-half mile east of Rock Key in 5 to 35 feet of water. Mooring buoys are provided. The Western Dry Docks are also shallow and also marked with buoys. Both have spur-and-groove coral formations. Both sites are SPAs.

While in the water, stop for a moment and float over one specific area. The longer you float and the longer you look, the more you will likely see: corals, fish, tiny shrimp, worms, and lobster. The diversity of species that reveals itself can be amazing (Plate 6).

At the Eastern Dry Docks one mooring buoy is not like the others. It is off by itself and surrounded by seagrass meadows on three sides. This is a good spot to find creatures like starfish and conchs.

The Western Dry Docks are farther away from Key West than the Eastern Dry Docks and consequently are less frequented by the local charter trade. For this reason, the western portion of the Dry Docks is considered a healthier marine environment.

GPS: Eastern Dry Docks: N 24 27.72 / W 81 50.86
Western Dry Docks: N 24 26.63 / W 81 55.61
Directions: 5 miles southwest of Key West.
Hours of Operation: n/a
Visitor Information: n/a
Web site: n/a
Boat Ramp: Key West Garrison Bight Marina, 1801 N. Roosevelt
    Blvd., 305.292.8167

25

Cottrell Key, Key West

Rating: Beginner to Advanced

Cottrell Key is named for an old salt named Cottrell whose job was to warn fellow sailors of the shallow reefs found here. Depths are from 3 to 15 feet. Mooring buoys mark the site. Cottrell Key is an SPA. When Atlantic waters are too rough to snorkel, Cottrell Key, found in the Gulf of Mexico and protected from adverse tidal conditions, is generally a calmer destination.

The small coral heads, sea fans, and sponges are west of the lighthouse. The shallow reef runs southwesterly in a straight line. Cottrell Key has many ledges where snapper, grouper, grunts, nurse sharks, and turtles seek cover. As with many of these shallow reefs, wrecks have occurred here. The only visible wreck site can be found near the buoy farthest east. During World War II, Cottrell Key was used as a practice target for fighter pilots and on occasion snorkelers can still find related artifacts.

GPS: N 25 36.20 / W 81 55.58
Directions: 8 miles west of Key West.
Hours of Operation: n/a
Visitor Information: n/a
Web site: n/a
Boat Ramp: Key West Garrison Bight Marina, 1801 N. Roosevelt
    Blvd., 305.292.8167

26

Marquesas Keys, Key West

Rating: Beginner to Advanced

The Marquesas are the only known atoll in the Atlantic. An atoll is a lagoon encompassed by a coral reef or a series of coral reefs. In the case of the Marquesas, a series of small exposed coral reefs and mangrove islets almost enclose a wide but shallow lagoon where depths range from 5 feet to over 100 feet.

Corals in these parts are all pretty much the same—brilliant and impressive. Because the Marquesas are a good stretch from Key West, the reefs are not as frequented as reefs found closer to the island, and for that reason, these are generally healthier than their counterparts. In addition, some of the larger islands boast impressive beaches that provide adequate anchorage for fabulous picnics as well as overnight or multiple-night stays.

The Marquesas are home to a number of wrecks. The Spanish treasure ship *Atocha* made a millionaire of the late Mel Fisher, a bona fide Florida Keys treasure hunter. Artifacts from this wreck, as well as others, are on display at his Key West museum.

Fishing captains cruise these flats in search of bonefish. When fishing for the elusive "gray ghost," captains push-pole their boats across the seagrass shallows as they scan for the tails of bonefish breaking through the surface. For those looking for extreme fly-fishing, fly poles are used to catch sharks in these waters.

GPS: N 24 31.69 / W 82 07.94
Directions: 25 miles west of Key West.
Hours of Operation: n/a
Visitor Information: n/a
Boat Ramp: Key West Garrison Bight Marina, 1801 N. Roosevelt
    Blvd., 305.292.8167

27

The Dry Tortugas, Key West

Rating: Beginner to Advanced

The Dry Tortugas were first called *Las Tortugas*, the Turtles, for the hordes of reptiles that once used the islands to bury their clutches of eggs. This collection of five islands was later renamed the Dry Tortugas as a way to inform passing sailing ships that the islands held no fresh water. The islands are a bit of a haul from civilization, but they represent some of the healthiest reefs Florida has to offer. Transportation to the Dry Tortugas is widely advertised in Key West and the trip can be made via boat or seaplane. Garden Key is the primary destination for sightseers, campers, and snorkelers. Camping is limited and available on a first-come, first-served basis.

The Dry Tortugas are best known for Fort Jefferson, originally constructed to protect Atlantic-bound trade ships traveling from the Mississippi River. The contrast of Fort Jefferson's emerald grass, variegated bricks, and sapphire sky can be breathtaking, as can the ruby-orange blooms of the Royal Poinciana trees inside Fort Jefferson's walls.

The fort was never fully constructed; 30 years after work began, the fort was made obsolete by the army. The only action the fort saw was as a Union military prison during the Civil War. Fort Jefferson's most distinguished resident was the infamous Dr. Mudd, who was indicted for conspiracy and harboring a fugitive, John Wilkes Booth. After Booth shot Abraham Lincoln, he jumped from the balcony at Ford's Theatre and broke his leg. Dr. Mudd, an acquaintance, set Booth's leg and, temporarily at least, gave him safe harbor.

From Garden Key, there is excellent snorkeling around the old dock jetties and along the outside of the moat wall. Bright sponges

Fort Jefferson: it's a long haul from Key West, but it's worth it.

and both hard and soft corals flourish in the shallow waters, as well as hordes of angelfish, butterflyfish, wrasses, and parrotfish. A great snorkeling wreck can be found offshore, though not within swimming distance of the fort. The Windjammer Wreck, or French Wreck, is often offered as an additional snorkeling site by charter boats; if you are offered the chance to snorkel here, take it. The

Windjammer sits in 18 feet of water, and at low tide, part of the ship still juts through the surface. This wreck is also home to the occasional Goliath grouper. This fish can reach the size of a circa 1970 VW Bug. The Windjammer wreck is a deeper site not recommended for snorkelers uncomfortable with diving below the surface.

The Dry Tortugas are also a principal resting and refueling ground for migrating birds. Popular with hard-core bird enthusiasts, the islands are the only place in America that trophy birds like sooty terns and brown boobies can be seen.

GPS: N 24 37.27 / W 82 56.58

Directions: 68 nautical miles west of Key West.

Hours of Operation: n/a

Visitor Information: 305.242.7700

Web site: www.nps.gov/drto

Boat Ramp: Key West Garrison Bight Marina, 1801 N. Roosevelt Blvd., 305.292.8167

Public Boat Ramps

Harry Harris Park
MM 92.5 O/S

Indian Key Fill
MM 79 B/S

Marathon
MM 54 B/S

Marathon Chamber of Commerce Yacht Club
MM 49 B/S

7-Mile Bridge
MM 40 B/S

Spanish Harbor
MM 34

Cudjoe Key
MM 20 B/S

Big Coppit Key
MM 11 O/S

Stock Island Ramp
MM 7 B/S

Key West Garrison Bight Marina
305.292.8167
1801 N. Roosevelt Blvd.

Key West Harbor
Simonton Street

Chambers of Commerce

More information can be obtained from the following chambers of commerce:

Key Largo
MM 106, Bayside
800.822.1088
www.keylargo.org

Islamorada
MM 83.2, Bayside
305.664.4503
www.islamoradachamber.com

Greater Marathon
MM 53.5, Bayside
305.743.5417
www.floridakeysmarathon.com

Lower Keys
MM 31, Oceanside
305.872.2411
www.lowerkeyschamber.com

Key West
402 Wall Street
305.294.2587
www.keywestchamber.org

Swimming with Dolphins

Dolphins Cove
MM 101.9, Bayside
877.365.2683
www.dolphinscove.com

Dolphins Plus
MM 100.5, Bayside
305.451.1993
www.dolphinsplus.com

Dolphin Research Center
MM 57, Bayside
305.289.0002

Hawk's Cay
MM 61, Oceanside
305.743.7000
www.hawkscay.com

Theater of the Sea
MM 84.5, Oceanside
305.664.2431
www.theaterofthesea.com

Chapter 2

Southeast Coastline

~~~~~~

For the purposes of this book, Southeast Florida encompasses an area of coastline that stretches between Homestead to the south and Sebastian Inlet to the north. A great many ships have wrecked in the shallows offshore and snorkelers can explore a number of them including the *Urca de Lima*, the *Breckonshire*, and the Cabin Wreck, found a few feet from the beach near the McLarty Treasure Museum in Sebastian. While this stretch of the coast does not claim the sugar-soft sands of the Panhandle or the clear blue waters and coral reefs of the Keys, traces of both can be found. Unlike the Keys, where natural sand beaches can seem harder to find than a suit and tie, beaches here stretch out for mile after undisturbed mile.

Because of the reef line's proximity to shore and its shallow nature, visibility can be greatly influenced by the tide. Snorkeling

~~~~~~

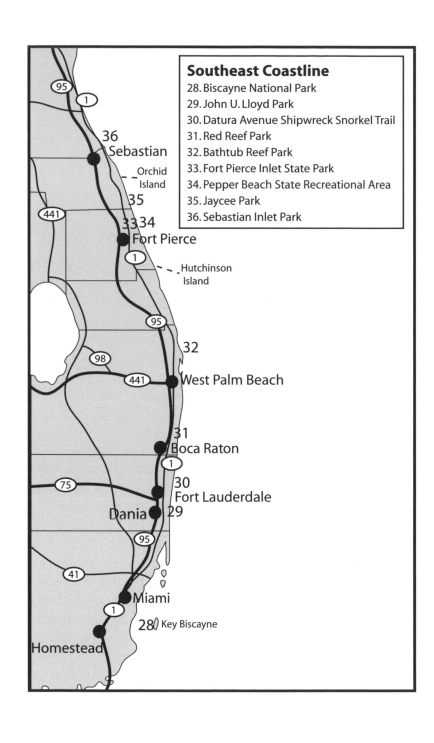

Southeast Coastline

28. Biscayne National Park
29. John U. Lloyd Park
30. Datura Avenue Shipwreck Snorkel Trail
31. Red Reef Park
32. Bathtub Reef Park
33. Fort Pierce Inlet State Park
34. Pepper Beach State Recreational Area
35. Jaycee Park
36. Sebastian Inlet Park

during the wrong tide can create conditions as different as night and day. Slack high tide is the optimum time to get into the water for two reasons. First, high tide brings in the clearer, bluer water found farther offshore, and second, at slack tide the water is still and sediment has a chance to settle to the bottom. Direct overhead sunlight will also increase the water's visibility; cloudy conditions will decrease it. Wind can affect visibility by producing choppy conditions, and surface chop translates into stirred bottom sediment.

Small-profile corals can be readily found within swimming distance from shore, and access to them is available from public beaches where lifeguards are often present. Lifeguards will sometimes be able to point out the general area of the first reef line. It is important to remember that snorkelers are not the only people using the water. People often fish from jetties and piers, so caution should always be a factor. While boats are not generally necessary to reach the wrecks and reef lines, boaters frequent the waters. Diver Down flags are, as always, imperative. You should take caution whenever you are exploring jetties. It is important to swim on the beach side of a jetty and not the inlet side where harsh currents can prove dangerous.

Above the Surface

The Everglades, first given national park status by President Roosevelt in 1934, are one of the reasons people travel from halfway around the world to visit South Florida. Named the "River of Grass" by Marjory Stoneman Douglas in 1947, the Everglades are a prairie of sawgrass wetlands and hardwood hammocks. Considered a major world ecosystem, the land is home to 25 kinds of orchids—including the rare ghost orchid—120 varieties of trees, 300 species of birds, and over 1,000 types of seed-bearing plants. Flocks of herons, egrets, and roseate spoonbills gather in the sawgrass river shallows to feed at dusk and dawn. Florida panthers roam the Everglades along with bobcats and alligators. From time to time, sightings of the elusive Swamp Ape are reported, though the veracity of these accounts is always questionable.

This land is a herpetological anomaly—it is the only place in the world where alligators and crocodiles co-exist. Because the Everglades are generally hot and muggy, the local fauna takes cover when the sun is strongest. The best times to visit the park are morning and late afternoon. Because of mosquitoes and biting flies, it is always good to visit the park armed with repellent. Sunscreen, hats, and cold water are also recommended. The Shark Valley visitor center offers a narrated 15-mile tram ride into the park. Cars are not permitted in this area.

The park has two main entrances: the Shark Valley entrance is between Naples and Miami on U.S. 41. The Florida City entrance can be found at the southernmost tip of Florida's Turnpike. Turn west at Palm Avenue and follow the road signs. Admission to the park is $10 per carload. For those staying in the area, the initial $10 fee allows the receipt holder access to the park for seven days.

South Florida is also the birthplace of one of the Sunshine State's original roadside attractions, alligator wrestling. To the first Floridians, alligator wrestling provided meat and leather for families. Before refrigeration, the best way to keep meat fresh was to keep it alive. Men, hunting alone, perfected techniques for capturing these wily reptiles. Referred to as bulldogging today, wrestling matches pitting man against beast are basic demonstrations of how an alligator can be captured and secured.

On the other side of the plate, alligator is commonly served in local restaurants. While frittered or fried might be its two most popular preparations, gator makes for a nice appetizer when sautéed with olive oil, butter, white wine, garlic, onion, salt, and pepper. Alligator jerky is common fare, and while most of the alligator's meat is taken from the tail, gator ribs are also occasionally served.

To see what true love looks like, visit the Coral Castle. A continuing mystery is how the 100-pound Latvian, Ed Leedskanlin, carved this coral masterpiece using tools crafted from the spare parts of a Model-T Ford. It took 28 years to complete and com-

Everglades Alligator Farm; don't try this at home.

prises over 1,000 tons of coral rock. The castle is furnished with nearly 100 tons of sculptures, including the 5,000-pound Feast of Love Table that was carved into a perfectly formed heart. Listed in Ripley's Believe It or Not, the table is featured as the World's Largest Valentine. The Coral Castle is in Homestead, at 28655 South Dixie Highway.

28

Biscayne National Park, Homestead

Rating: Beginner to Advanced

If you don't want to travel south the extra 40 minutes it takes to reach Key Largo, Biscayne National Park is the best spot to snorkel over coral reefs similar to those found in the Keys. Like John Pennekamp Coral Reef State Park, most of Biscayne National Park is underwater. The Dante Fascell Visitor Center offers exhibits depicting examples of the flora and fauna found in coral reef, key, bay, and mangrove communities.

Canoe and kayak rentals are available for snorkelers or anyone else who wants to explore the lush seagrass meadows surrounding the park. In addition to snorkeling charters, tickets to the glass-bottom boat tour over the reefs are available at the visitor center, which is open every day except Christmas, weather permitting.

For reef diving, the hot spot in the park is Ball Buoy Reef (GPS: N 25 19.097 / W 80 11.059); this shallow reef lies in less than 20 feet of water and is richly adorned with hard and soft corals including elkhorn corals and seafans. Another popular snorkeling site in the park is the wreck of the *Mandalay* (GPS: N 25 26.530 / W 80 07.301), a 128-foot steel schooner—once a part of the Windjammer cruise line—that sank on New Year's Eve in 1966. The ship lies in water less than 15 feet deep and has been encrusted with both hard and soft corals. On windy or choppy days, when the water is too rough to snorkel open water sites like the *Mandalay* or Ball Buoy Reef, try Sandwich Cove (GPS: N 25 25.000 / W 80 13.000). This is a protected area that will give snorkelers a chance to experience some of Florida's colorful marine life.

Beyond the visitor center and surrounding picnic area, the majority of the park is accessible only by boat. Public boat ramps from Crandon Park on Key Biscayne to Homestead's Bayfront Park are located close enough to the park to explore not only the park's shallow reefs but also Elliot Key (which has restrooms), Boca Chita, and Adams Key. Picnicking and overnight camping are available on these islands, and all provide grills and picnic tables. Fresh water must be packed in and trash packed out.

Address: 9700 SW 928, Homestead.
Directions: From the Florida Turnpike, drive east on SW 328 (North Canal Street) for approximately 9 miles.
Hours of Operation: 7:00 a.m. to 5:00 p.m., 365 days a year.
Visitor Information: 305.230.7275
Web site: www.nps.gov/bisc/

Dive boat, Biscayne National Park.

29

John U. Lloyd Beach State Park, Dania Beach

Rating: Beginner to Advanced

With 251 acres of land and over two miles of beach, this park is an excellent place to escape the hurried pace of the city. The park was named after John U. Lloyd, an attorney who served Broward County for 30 years. John U. Lloyd Beach is a sea turtle nesting ground annually producing as many as 10,000 hatchlings. Beer,

John U. Lloyd Beach, Fort Lauderdale.

wine, food, and bait are available at the Loggerhead Café. The park provides restroom facilities as well as grills and picnic tables.

The first reef line grows in 10 to 15 feet of water; park in either the Number 1 or 2 parking lots. Lobster and small tropicals like porgys and sergeant majors can be found hiding in crevices. Eels, rays, and small nurse sharks can also be seen on occasion.

Canoe and kayak rentals are available at the park if you are in the mood for a paddle. Travel down Whiskey Creek, a mangrove-lined water trail flowing through the park that was once used to smuggle booze during Prohibition. Manatees frequent the creek, which is also said to be haunted by a specter called the Red-Eyed Lady.

Should the beach or the snorkeling area be too packed for your taste, travel to nearby Dania Beach Park, which is at 100 North Beach Road, immediately south of the park. Snorkelers can access the reef line by swimming out from the south end of the beach.

Address: 6503 N. Ocean Drive, Dania Beach.
Directions: Florida Turnpike to Hollywood Blvd, Exit 49; east to
    A1A; north 2.5 miles.
Hours of Operation: 8:00 a.m. until sundown, 365 days a year.
Visitor Information: 954.923.2833
Web site: www.floridastateparks.org/lloydbeach/

30

Datura Avenue Shipwreck Snorkel Trail, Lauderdale-by-the-Sea

Rating: Intermediate to Advanced

With the help of Jean-Michel Cousteau, the Shipwreck Snorkel Trail was dedicated in May 2002. The Shipwreck Snorkel Trail is not really a trail nor is it really a shipwreck. The planted debris replicates an early 1800s shipwreck that has been thoughtfully laid out in approximately 18 feet of water. This compact site is bordered to the north by two concrete replica cannons and to the south by three replica cannons. In addition to a pile of ballast stones, there is an 11-foot anchor.

Start by standing on the beach directly in front of the Datura Street entrance. Locate the white buoy floating offshore. Swimming out to the buoy, you will find the site laid out 150 feet to the east and 150 feet to the west. The ballast stone pile has a cache of nooks and crannies where critters can hide. Take a deep breath and swim down for a closer look. Colorful tropicals, small crabs, shrimp, and at least one eel call these rocks home.

This is a popular site among both snorkelers and divers, so parking can be limited. Parking is strictly metered; bring five quarters for every hour you plan to spend. This snorkel is recommended for strong swimmers who are comfortable in the water.

Address: The intersection of Datura Avenue and the beach.
Directions: From I-95 take the Commercial Boulevard Exit east;
    south on A1A; east on Datura Avenue; east to the beach.
Hours of Operation: n/a
Visitor Information: n/a
Web site: n/a

Plate 1. Queen angelfish.

WEC2006100901

Plate 2. The mysterious *fibropapilloma* disease.

Plate 3. Pork fish.

Plate 4. Cushion star found in a seagrass bed near Indian Key.

Plate 5. Christmas tree worms.

Plate 6. Hogfish.

Plate 7. Nurse shark.

Plate 8. The beautiful
Rainbow River.

Plate 9. Mermaid with manatee at Weeki Wachee Springs.

Plate 10. Head spring at Rainbow Springs.

Plate 11. Atlantic spadefish.

Plate 12. Southern stingray.

Plate 13. Sea rods.

Plate 14. Spotted eagle ray.

Plate 15. Queen angelfish.

Plate 16. Pufferfish.

31

Red Reef Park, Boca Raton

Rating: Beginner to Advanced

This 67-acre oceanfront park is another perfect site for a family escape. Picnic areas, showers, and bathroom facilities are available. Parking can run as high as $15. Lifeguards are on duty from 9 a.m. to 5 p.m. throughout the year. As well as snorkeling opportunities, there is a fishing pier and plenty of room to unfold a beach towel and breathe in the warm salt air. This is a great site for younger snorkelers.

Snorkeling is done from the south end of the park. Rock structures can be found right off the beach in shallows from 3 to 6 feet

Gumbo-limbo tree, also called the tourist tree.

deep. Colorful sponges, blue and yellow striped grunts, and small schools of snappers can be spotted. Small nurse sharks, southern stingrays, and eels are occasional visitors (Plate 7). For those looking for optimum conditions, visit the park at slack high tide.

After your snorkel, be sure to see a gumbo-limbo. The gumbo-limbo is a native tree; it is sometimes called a tourist tree because its thin red layer of bark is always peeling away from its trunk the way the skin of sunburned tourists seems to. The Gumbo Limbo Environmental Education Center, at 1801 N. Ocean Boulevard, offers boardwalk strolls through a natural coastal hammock. Marine tanks house some of the local underwater residents. The tanks are great fun for children of all ages. There is no fee associated with the center.

Address: 1400 N. State Road A1A, Boca Raton.
Directions: From I-95, take the Palmetto Park Road exit east to
    A1A; north on A1A for approximately 1 mile.
Hours of Operation: Daily from 8:00 a.m. to 10 p.m.
Visitor Information: 561.393.7974
Web site: www.ci.boca-raton.fl.us/parks/redreef.cfm

32

Bathtub Reef Park, Stuart

Rating: Beginner to Advanced

The park is found at the south end of Hutchinson Island. Restroom and showering facilities are available and lifeguards are on duty from morning through the afternoon. Arrive early if you plan to

Bathtub Reef Park, a wonderful snorkeling spot for children.

visit on weekends as the sand parking lot fills rapidly. There is no fee for parking. This site is called Bathtub Reef because the reef structure creates water conditions that can be absolutely calm and serene. The result is an ideal snorkel for the entire family.

The reef structure is less than a 100-foot swim from the beach and is shallow, with depths ranging from 2 to 15 feet. At low tide the reef becomes exposed. At high tide, snorkelers are able to swim over the top of the reef, where urchins, crabs, and snails can be found in the crevices. Colorful tropicals like parrotfish can be found as well as the occasional angelfish, grouper, and snook.

Follow the boardwalk to several large posters that tell the complete story of the reef, which is called a worm reef. It was built by small marine worms called *Sabellariid* worms that ingest sand and excrete a sticky substance that has, over time, hardened to create the reef.

Gilbert's Bar House of Refuge can be found near the park and is the oldest building on the Treasure Coast. It is also a museum. In the nineteenth century, six houses of refuge lined the coastline. The houses were set up to give shipwrecked sailors who washed ashore a place to get a warm meal, a little rum, and a bed for the night. In addition to being a historical monument, the building still acts as a refuge for a different seafaring species. Hatchling sea turtles are reared here before being released into the wild.

Address: 1585 SE MacArthur Boulevard, Stuart.
Directions: From I-95, take Exit 62, SR714, east to Stuart; right on
     East Ocean Boulevard; right on MacArthur Boulevard.
Hours of Operation: Sunrise to sunset.
Visitor Information: n/a
Web site: n/a

33

Fort Pierce Inlet State Park, Fort Pierce

Rating: Intermediate to Advanced

This 340-acre park has a one-half-mile-long beach that is adorned with sea oats, coastal hammocks, and nature trails. Bathrooms and picnic facilities are provided, and the fee for parking is nominal. Because the small-profile reef line is a fairly good swim from the beach, this site is not recommended for beginning snorkelers or children. Park in either the number 1 or number 2 parking lots.

Between 200 and 300 feet offshore, a small-profile reef structure runs the length of the beach in 15 to 30 feet of water. The jetty here provides a good structure around which fish can gather. Be sure

Fort Pierce Inlet State Park.

to give a wide berth to those areas where people are fishing. Also, swim on the beach side of the jetty and not the channel side where ripping currents can be hazardous. Diver Down flags are essential. The water can be choppy when the weather is windy, so take this into consideration before diving in. Remember, choppy water makes for poor visibility.

Another site you might want to check out is nearby Avalon Park, 5 miles north of Fort Pierce Inlet State Park. As well as the reefline, World War II relics in the water create excellent artificial structures to explore. For those hoping to get a good look at a sea cow, visit the Manatee Observation Education Center in Fort Pierce, which offers lookout points with telescopes as well as eco-tours through the Indian River Lagoon.

Address: 905 Shorewinds Dr., Fort Pierce.
Directions: 4 miles east of Fort Pierce on North Causeway.
Hours of Operation: 8 a.m. to sunset, 365 days a year.
Visitor Information: 772.468.3985
Web site: www.floridastateparks.org/fortpierceinlet/

34

Pepper Beach State Recreational Area, Fort Pierce

Rating: Intermediate to Advanced

Pepper Park is fully loaded with picnic, shower, and bathroom facilities, as well as a series of courts used for basketball, volleyball, and tennis. There are lifeguards, playgrounds for the children, picnic facilities, and grills. For beachside lounging, the sand stretches for an entire mile. The small-profile reef line is 300 feet offshore and probably not suited for younger snorkelers. For those willing to take the swim, both soft and hard corals can be found as well as the usual reef creatures including sergeant majors, snappers, lobster, and southern stingrays. You must have a Diver Down flag with you.

Three hundred feet beyond the first reef line lies the wreck of the *Urca de Lima*, an eighteenth-century Spanish sailing vessel, in 10–15 feet of water. The *Urca de Lima* (GPS: N 27 26.65 / W 80 10.28) was one of the ships lost in the hurricane of 1715. To find her walk north up the beach, past a wooded lot and the Bauman Apartments. Continue a few hundred feet north of the apartments and swim out.

Should you arrive by boat, a limited number of marker buoys are available. Should they be occupied, remember to toss your anchor in an open sandy spot where its settling will do no harm.

After snorkeling over the remains of the *Urca de Lima*, visit the McLarty Treasure Museum at Sebastian Inlet State Park to see some of the artifacts salvaged from the wreck.

Address: 2300 North A1A, Fort Pierce.
Directions: From SR A1A, the park is 2.5 miles south of the Indian
    River County line.

Hours of Operation: Dawn to dusk.
Visitor Information: 772.462.1521
Web site: n/a

35

Jaycee Park, Vero Beach

Rating: Intermediate to Advanced

This park has a full load of facilities including restrooms, showers, lifeguards, and a playground for the kids. Two reef lines can be found off the beach of Jaycee Park. The first lies about 200 feet offshore in 10 to 20 feet of water. Lobsters and eels can be spotted at the reef line as well as tangs, surgeonfish, and the ever-present sergeant major.

For more intrepid snorkelers, a second reef line runs about 400 feet beyond the first. Make sure your dive flag is clearly visible. The difference between the first and second reef lines is that the second reef line will generally have more complex schools of fish and better-defined coral formations.

Experienced snorkelers can also access a different part of the small reef line from the Conn Beach Board Walk adjacent to the park. The reef line runs about 600 feet offshore in 15–20 feet of water. The best time to reach the corals is at slack high tide when the clearer waters from farther offshore have pushed in.

Address: 4200 Ocean Drive, Vero Beach.
Directions: A1A to Ocean Drive, turn east.
Hours of Operation: Sunrise to sunset.
Visitor Information: 772.231.0578
Web site: n/a

36

Sebastian Inlet State Park, Sebastian

Rating: Beginner to Advanced

This park comes replete with amenities including camping, food concessions, fishing piers, and canoe and kayak rentals. The park never closes and encompasses 3 miles of beach. Two museums are located on the property: the Sebastian Fishing Museum and the McLarty Treasure Museum. The park is not only a fishing hot spot but also the site of major surf contests.

The McLarty Treasure Museum is dedicated to the ill-fated Spanish treasure fleet of 1715 and, reportedly, sits on the site of a shipwreck survivor's campsite. The Cabin Wreck (GPS: N 27 49.80 / W 80 25.54), thought to be the *Nuesta de la Regala*, can be found in the shallows off the wall of rocks at the north end of the McLarty Treasure Museum. The wreck site has cannons, anchors, and ballast piles and rests in 5 to 20 feet of water. For the best water visibility, snorkel this site at slack high tide.

Children will enjoy snorkeling in the tidal pool on the north side of the park. During slack tide, more experienced snorkelers can explore the inlet, although this can be a dangerous enterprise. Boat traffic can be heavy, and the turn of the tide can make swimming treacherous. Dive flags are imperative. More experienced snorkelers should swim near the catwalk beneath the bridge. Be careful of fisherman!

To the south of the park is Pelican Island, the first National Wildlife Refuge in the United States. The 5-acre mangrove island is a roosting site for pelicans as well as other species including egrets and herons. President Theodore Roosevelt established the refuge in 1903 as a way of helping to protect bird species suffering duress from the feather trade of the 1900s.

Address: 9700 South A1A, Sebastian.
Directions: I-95 to US192, exit east to SR A1A, turn right.
Hours of Operation: 24 hours a day, 365 days a year.
Visitor Information: 321.984.4852
Web site: www.floridastateparks.org/sebastianinlet/

Chambers of Commerce

More information can be obtained from the following chambers
of commerce:

Boca Raton
1800 N. Dixie Hwy.
561.395.4433
www.bocaratonchamber.com

Dania Beach
102 W. Dania Beach Blvd.
954.926.2323
www.greaterdania.org

Homestead/Florida City
43 N. Krome Ave.
305.247.2332

Fort Pierce
2200 Virginia Ave.
772.595.9999
www.stluciechamber.org
www.chamberinaction.com

Fort Lauderdale
512 NE 3rd Ave.
954.462.6000
www.ftlchamber.com

Lauderdale-by-the-Sea
4201 Ocean Dr.
954.776.1000
www.lbts.com

Miami
1601 Biscayne Blvd.
305.305.7700
www.greatermiami.com/

Sebastian
700 Main St.
772.589.5969
www.sebastianchamber.com

Stuart
1650 S. Kanner Hwy.
772.287.1088
www.goodnature.org

Vero Beach
1216 21st St.
772.567.3491
www.indianriverchamber.com

Chapter 3

Springs and Rivers

At a regular 72 degrees, spring water is considered cold by some and refreshing by others. For snorkelers, wetsuits are recommended. Florida's springs are brilliant, beautiful pools shimmering with shades of turquoise, emerald, and blue. Often they are crested with delicately fringed ferns and hardwoods draped with Spanish moss (Plate 8). Snorkelers will love them for their clarity, as pure spring water is clear as a gin martini.

There is a quiet beauty beneath the surface. Schools of bream huddle under the crippled limbs of fallen cypress trees, while snapping turtles and red-eared sliders swim doggedly through the water. Long-whiskered catfish chin their way along the bottom, and garfish, like legless alligators, float as still as logs at the surface.

Over 500 natural springs make up the Sunshine State's spring system, the largest of its kind in the world. Collectively, Florida's springs expel in excess of 19 billion gallons of fresh water every day. Springs come in different sizes, from small puddles the size of a hot tub to grand Olympic-sized pools.

Springs are classified by the amount, or magnitude, of water they expel on a daily basis. The most powerful class of spring is called a first-magnitude spring and produces at least 65 million gallons of

Snorkeling with manatee at King's River in Homosassa.

water per day, which, for those trying to comprehend the amount, is enough water to fill about 100 Olympic-sized swimming pools. Florida has 33 first-magnitude springs and 70 second-magnitude springs. The lowest magnitude spring is an eighth-magnitude spring, which produces less than one pint of water per minute, or less than 15,000 gallons of water per day.

Florida's spring system is also considered manatee country. Unlike other marine mammals such as the walrus or whale, manatees do not have a thick layer of blubber insulating them against the cold. Manatees are a thin-skinned species capable of succumbing to the cold when water temperatures dip below 68 degrees. For this reason, during fall and winter months, much of Florida's manatee population migrates to this elaborate spring system.

Though unrelated to the cow, manatees are commonly referred to as sea cows. They are, after all, somewhat bovine in shape and manner. Biologically speaking, the manatee is most closely related to the elephant and, as a matter of reasoning, should be referred to

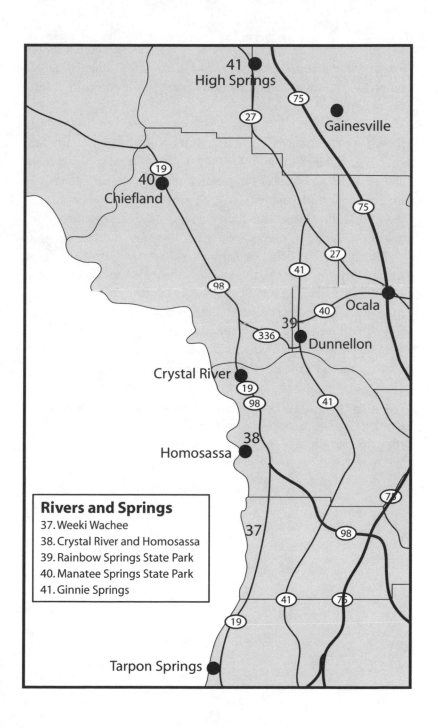

41
High Springs

75

27

Gainesville

19

40
Chiefland

75

27

98

41

40 Ocala

39

336 Dunnellon

Crystal River

19

98

41

38
Homosassa

Rivers and Springs
37. Weeki Wachee
38. Crystal River and Homosassa
39. Rainbow Springs State Park
40. Manatee Springs State Park
41. Ginnie Springs

37

75

98

41

75

19

Tarpon Springs

as a sea elephant. Adults can grow to 12 feet in length and weigh in excess of 1,000 pounds. Voracious salad eaters, an adult will nibble down 100 pounds of greens, including seagrass and water hyacinth, every day.

Towns like Crystal River and Homosassa swell with snorkelers seeking to experience a close encounter with a manatee. The Marine Mammal Protection Act of 1972 makes it illegal to harass manatees, whales, otters, sea lions, seals, and dolphins. Illegal manatee interaction includes approaching, chasing, thumping, striking, tugging, and riding them (considered having two hands on the animal at any one time); manatees are neither toys nor amusements.

Manatees are a social species and will approach people. Should a manatee approach you, the interaction is not considered harassment. Still, when this is the case, show restraint. Gently stroke the manatee or scratch its belly. Manatees are a gentle species; do not tug or pull on them. When the manatee has had enough it will swim away, and by law, you must allow the animal to do so.

The handful of springs included here are not the only places snorkelers might dip in. If you are seeking a spontaneous adventure, drive along highways 19 or 27, as both roads wind through the heart of spring country. No sooner do you drive past one spring than you see the sign for another posted in the grasses bordering the road.

37

Weeki Wachee Springs

Rating: Beginner to Advanced

Weeki Wachee is Seminole for "Little Spring." However, there is nothing little about a first-magnitude spring that expels 170 million gallons of fresh water every day. In fact, the bottom of the spring has never been found. The modern-day facilities at Weeki Wachee are the creation of a man named Newton Perry who trained Navy SEALs during World War II. Newton arrived at the spring in 1946, built an underwater theater into the side of the spring, and hired a group of performing mermaids to entertain live audiences.

In 1947, the theater was 6 feet below the surface and seated a dozen people; today, the theater sits 16 feet below the surface of the spring and seats 500 people. In addition to the mermaid show, the natural spring features a water park, river cruise, picnic areas, kiddie pool, and tiki bar. During warmer summer months, snorkelers will appreciate the clarity of the water at Buccaneer Bay, as well as the cool respite it offers. For those sensitive to cold water, wetsuits are never a bad idea. In addition to the occasional mermaid, you can see otters, manatees, turtles, and fish (Plate 9).

Once upon a time the mermaids of Weeki Wachee carried as much clout as the mouse does up in Orlando and attracted fans the likes of Elvis and Don Knotts. The mermaids perform twice daily and have been known to drink, eat, perform ballets, and play football underwater. For children, the park offers a two-day Mermaid Camp where participants are educated in the ways of a mermaid's life both on and off stage. These junior mermaids also get to perform in one of the live mermaid shows.

Address: 6131 Commercial Way, Weeki Wachee.
Directions: At the crossroads of US 19 and State Road 50, one hour north of Tampa.

Hours of Operation: Seasonal. Summer Hours: Monday through
Friday, 10 a.m. to 4 p.m.; Saturday and Sunday, 10 a.m. to 5 p.m.
Winter hours vary.
Visitor Information: 352.596.2062
Web site: www.weekiwachee.com

38

Crystal River and Homosassa

Rating: Beginner to Advanced

For those who want to snorkel with a sea cow, manatee eco-tours are a way of life in the towns of Crystal River and Homosassa. During winter months when water temperatures begin dipping, nearly one-quarter of the Florida manatee population heads to one of the many springs feeding both the Homosassa and Crystal rivers. Homosassa is referred to as the Manatee Capital of the World. Probably, the only reason Crystal River doesn't claim this title is because the Homosassa town council hatched the idea first. Manatees, as well as manatee snorkeling tours, are taken seriously in this part of the state. Locating a facility offering a manatee snorkeling tour will be about as difficult as buying a cup of coffee.

Stop by either town's Chamber of Commerce for handfuls of rack cards advertising Swim with the Manatee Eco-Tours. For those who want to create their own adventure, driving through either town will also produce a great many opportunities to rent canoes or kayaks. Spotting a manatee on your own is not difficult. These are large animals, in excess of 10 feet in length and as big as cows. Should you be out on your own and spot a roped-off area, do not cross the line as sanctuary areas have been set up to protect these gentle beasts.

Charter boat operations take snorkelers out on manatee encounter adventures two and sometimes three times a day—they start early, generally by 8 a.m. For later risers the early afternoon trip will offer an identical package. The big difference, however, is that the chances the captain will actually locate a willing manatee are greater first thing in the morning when the manatees are just waking up.

Pontoon boat, Crystal River.

Both Crystal River and Homosassa are havens for manatee collectables. For those in search of souvenirs, mugs, rugs, T-shirts, placemats, stuffed animals, hats, picture frames, shot glasses, calendars, and videos are available, as well as anything else you might imagine. The Citrus County Manatee Festival has been held in Crystal River every January for the past 20 years.

Like all spring swims, this is a cold but awesome adventure. However you choose to have a manatee encounter, remember that it is against the law to approach or harass the animal. The manatee must approach you for the interaction not to be considered harassment.

Address: Route 19.
Directions: Homosassa is around 75 miles north of Tampa and
    Crystal River is 8 miles north of Homosassa.
Hours of Operation: n/a
Visitor Information: Homosassa: 352.628.2666; Crystal River:
    352.795.3149
Web site: n/a

39

Rainbow Springs State Park, Dunnellon

Rating: Beginner to Advanced

Rainbow Springs is a first-magnitude spring that expels more than 400 million gallons of water every day, making it Florida's fourth largest spring. The waterfalls found around the lush confines of the park are man-made remnants of an earlier time when Rainbow Springs was a bona fide roadside attraction. Picnic areas are available as are restrooms, food concessions, camping facilities, and canoe and kayak rentals. Admission to the park is $1.

Snorkeling is allowed in the roped-off swimming area of the park but not over the headspring unless the snorkelers are accompanied by a park ranger (Plate 10). Rangers conduct snorkeling tours and will explain a little about the history, flora, and fauna. Rainbow Springs has created the Rainbow River. With little to no current, depths not exceeding 7 feet, and crystal clear waters spilling out from its source spring, the Rainbow River is one of the best river run snorkels in the state. Boats frequent the river and dive flags are imperative. You can swim for miles up and down the river, and along the way you will find several smaller springs to explore. The start of the river is off limits to boats, though canoes and kayaks are permitted to explore the area. Swimming is not allowed at the head of the river.

For those not staying at the park's campground, access to the river is also possible at K. P. Hole Park, located just south of the state park. Snorkelers can wade in from a sandy beach area; canoe and kayak rentals are available. Boat owners can use the public ramp to launch. K. P. Hole Park is located down the first road on the left as you leave Rainbow Springs State Park.

After a leisurely snorkel, why not kick back with an inner tube and float down the river? While those who are camping in the park

will be allowed access inside the camp boundaries, those without this access can launch their tubes at K. P. Hole County Park,
352.489.3055. It takes about four hours to slowly drift down the
river—a great way to spend a hot summer afternoon.

Rainbow Springs was once a roadside attraction. Instead of offering the usual glass-bottom boat ride, the Rainbow Springs attraction used submarine boats to ferry passengers through the
water, giving them a fish-eye's view. In 1990, the state saved the
land from residential development by purchasing it and creating
Rainbow Springs State Park.

Address: 19158 S.W. 81st Pl. Rd, Dunnellon.
Directions: From I-75, take the second Ocala exit to SR 40 going
    west; turn left on US 41; the park will be on the left-hand side.
Hours of Operation: 8:00 a.m. to sundown, 365 days a year.
Visitor Information: 352.465.8555
Web site: www.floridastateparks.org/rainbowsprings/

40

Manatee Springs State Park, Chiefland

Rating: Beginner to Advanced

Manatee Springs is a first-magnitude spring pumping out over 100 million gallons of water every day; the water temperature is a steady 72 degrees year round. A staircase leads into the water. As the park is a bit removed from the rest of the world, cell phones do not work very well there, which may, depending on your point of view, be a good thing. Restroom facilities, grills, and picnic areas are available, as are food and drink concessions during summer months.

Enter the turquoise waters at the staircase and investigate the main spring before swimming down a short run to the Suwannee River. The water in the run does not get deeper than 8 feet and while boats are not permitted, canoes and kayaks are. To ensure your safety, dive flags are required. Bass, bream, mullet, and turtles can be spotted.

During fall and winter months, when the Gulf waters begin to chill, manatees seek out the warmer spring waters. Should you encounter one of these docile creatures, remember that it is unlawful to approach or harass them. While manatees frequently approach snorkelers, often they don't. There are times when, for whatever the reason, they do not feel in the mood. If the animal does not approach you, don't swim over and grab at it. If it appears disinterested in you, respect its desire for solitude.

For those looking to squeeze in two snorkel excursions in one day, after Manatee Springs, visit nearby Fanning Springs. This shallow spring is less than 20 feet deep and offers steps leading into the water for easy access. Fanning Springs State Park is just outside the town of Fanning Springs. From U.S. 19, take the second left after crossing the Suwannee River bridge. Fanning Springs State

Park is at 18020 NW Highway 19. For visitor information, call 352.463.3420.

Address: 11650 N.W. 115th St., Chiefland.

Directions: From US 98/19, drive west on Highway 320 for approximately 6 miles.

Hours of Operation: 8:00 a.m. to sundown, 365 days a year.

Visitor Information: 352.493.6072

Web site: www.floridastateparks.org/manateesprings/

41

Ginnie Springs Outdoors, High Springs

Rating: Beginner to Advanced

Ginnie Springs is one of the more popular Florida springs and offers a convenient snorkeling experience. Ginnie Springs Outdoors is a complete diving and snorkeling camping resort, leaving little to want on afternoon or weekend visits. For day visitors, the entrance fee is $10 for adults and $3 for children 7–14; the fee is waived for those who are younger. No lifeguards are present. Snorkeling gear, canoes, kayaks, and inner tube rentals are available onsite. Ginnie Springs is a second-magnitude spring and contributes, along with several other area springs, to the Sante Fe River. Three hundred campsites are available on a first come, first served basis.

There are several springs in the area, and each has a wooden staircase leading into the water. You can investigate individual springs or snorkel the whole collection by starting at one of the three Devil springs and snorkeling down the lazy currents of the Sante Fe River. Along the way you will find Ginnie, Dogwood, Twin, and Deer springs. This is not a labor-intensive sojourn, and you can finish your trip at any spring. None is a far walk back to your starting point. While the springs themselves will always be crystal clear, during winter and spring months, the water in the Sante Fe can become cloudy. Water visibility clears during summer and early fall. You must have a dive flag present when snorkeling in the river because recreational boaters frequent these waters.

For those who are camping overnight, the springs are lit by overhead lights that create a rare opportunity for night snorkeling. Once the sun goes down, snorkeling beneath the moon and stars can make for an unearthly experience. There will be a lot to look at, including eels, crayfish, turtles, and big bass out on the prowl. Lights are turned off at 1:00 a.m.

After snorkeling, grab an inner tube, slide into the water, and float down the Sante Fe. Bring your own tube or rent one at the Country Store. Enter at Devil Spring and float downstream to the take-out at Twin Springs. The leisurely trip will take about one hour. The walk back will take about 15 minutes.

Address: 7300 NE Ginnie Springs Road, High Springs.
Directions: From I-75, exit 399 west to US441-N, left on SR27/41, right on CR 340, north on NE 60th Avenue.
Hours: 8:00 a.m. to 6:00 p.m. during winter months and 8:00 a.m. to 8:00 p.m. during daylight savings time.
Visitor Information: 386.454.7188
Web site: www.ginniespringsoutdoors.com

Chambers of Commerce

More information can be obtained from the following chambers of commerce:

Chiefland
23 SE 2nd Ave.
352.493.1849
www.chieflandchamber.com

Crystal River
28 NW Hwy. 19
352.795.3149
www.citruscountychamber.com

Dunnellon
20500 E. Pennsylvania Ave.
352.489.2320
www.dunnellonchamber.org

High Springs
25 NE Railroad Ave.
386.454.3120
www.highsprings.com

Homosassa
3495 S. Suncoast Blvd.
352.628.2666

Chapter 4

Panhandle Beaches

Florida's Panhandle is a snorkeler's delight, and much of the credit goes to the Appalachian Mountains. Over the course of one billion years, time and river currents have whittled away at the mountain range and washed its particles downstream to the Gulf of Mexico. By the time the Appalachian dust has settled on to the floor of the Gulf, it has been reduced to pure quartz crystal that becomes sand as soft as margarita salt. It crunches underfoot when you walk across it.

The quartz sediment on the bottom of the Gulf also reflects the sun back toward the surface, thus enhancing the water's clarity; it is the clear blue of a backyard swimming pool. Up and down the beaches, the bobbing heads of snorkelers dot the shallows. While this is some of the clearest water in the state, structure can be hard to find.

The sites listed in this section all have prominent structures for snorkelers to explore. Many of these come in the form of rock jetties. Whenever you are snorkeling along jetties, take the time to look into the nooks and crannies for signs of life. Like seagrass beds, many of the species calling these rocky areas home make it a habit to blend in with their environment.

On the other end of the spectrum, because the Gulf of Mexico's 100-fathom line drifts relatively close to shore, species regularly seen in deeper waters, including sea turtles, dolphins, and manta rays, will occasionally be spotted close to shore. While the wingspan of an adult manta ray can stretch as many as 18 feet across, these impressive specimens are not as common in the shallows close to shore as are the schools of their much smaller offspring. Manta rays are sometimes referred to as "devil fish" because of what appear to be two horny structures sticking out of their heads. Mantas can be monstrous in size, but they are as harmless as they are graceful.

Like most Floridians, the tropical fish that can be found here, including damselfish and gobies, prefer their water warm and generally come inshore after the water temperatures rise for the summer (Plate 11). Although snorkeling along the Panhandle is not necessarily a seasonal activity, the water does get a little chilly in the winter.

Above the Surface

Florida's Panhandle has a lot to see above the surface, too. The small town of Gulf Breeze, located east of Pensacola, reports more sightings of unidentified flying objects than any other place in the country. In fact, some consider Gulf Breeze the UFO capital of the world. Without necessarily debunking any theories, we should note that two U.S. military posts are stationed near Gulf Breeze: Elgin Air Force Base and the Pensacola Naval Air Station, both of which are known to fly top-secret experimental aircraft.

The Flora-Bama Lounge straddles the state lines of Alabama and Florida. Jimmy Buffett sings about the Flora-Bama Lounge, a classic Florida beach bar that has been around for as long as anyone seems to remember. The bar is also home to the annual Interstate Mullet Toss where, since 1961, people have gathered on the last weekend in April to see how far they can throw a dead mullet over the state line; wearing gloves is prohibited.

Jetties attract myriads of marine life.

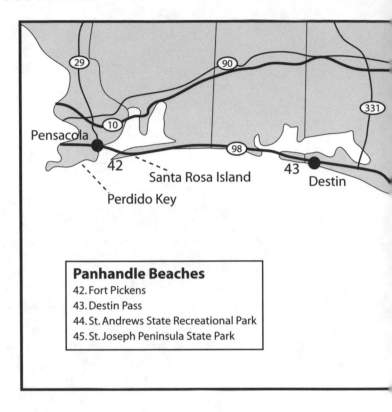

Panhandle Beaches
42. Fort Pickens
43. Destin Pass
44. St. Andrews State Recreational Park
45. St. Joseph Peninsula State Park

Amusement seekers will have their hearts filled to the brim in Panama City, where arcades, thrill rides, bungee jumping, and the original putt-putt golf, Goofy Golf, line Highway 98. For those desiring peace and quiet, note that Panama City feels like Spring Break—even in the summer.

South of Port St. Joe, tupelo gum trees flourish along the Chipola and Apalachicola rivers. In spring, when the trees flower, bees harvest their nectar. Back at the hive, they generate tupelo honey, considered the champagne of honey. This is the only place in America that tupelo honey is commercially harvested, during a period that lasts only 14 days every year. The Tupelo Honey Festival is held each May in the town of Wewahitchka.

Anyone who appreciates a good oyster, perhaps the best oyster ever tasted, should make it a point to stop at Boss Oyster in

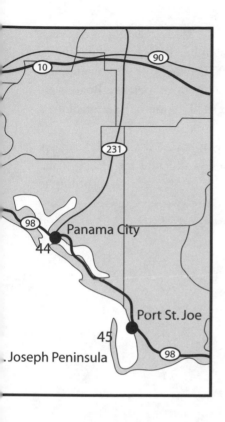

Apalachicola. Raw oysters, served plump, firm, and icy cold, is one option, though not the only one. The restaurant offers two pages of oyster toppings including Ceviche, Cubano, and Rockefeller II, featuring bacon, spinach, and smoked Gouda cheese.

Speaking of bivalve mollusks, the scallops found in this part of the state have tender mouth-watering meat and are excellent sautéed with olive oil, butter, and garlic. Add diced green peppers, onions, a dash of fresh ground pepper, and a pinch of salt, pour over al dente pasta, sprinkle with fresh basil and parmesan cheese, and you have created a feast.

Once upon a time, healthy populations of scallops could be found from Pensacola to West Palm Beach. This is not the case today. The recreational harvesting of scallops is allowed in the Gulf of Mexico only from the south bank of the Suwannee River to the

Mexico Beach canal. Open season for the harvesting of bay scallops runs from July 1 through September 10. Harvesting must be done either by hand or with a net. The bag limit is two gallons of scallops in the shell, or 1 pint of scallop meat, per day. Boaters are allowed 10 gallons of scallops in the shell or one-half gallon of meat per boat.

Scallop Day on St. Joseph Bay happens on the first Saturday of September (Labor Day weekend) at Frank Pate Park. What Apalachicola is to oysters, scallops are to Port St. Joe, and according to local lore, the waters here produce the sweetest, juiciest scallops this side of the moon.

42

Fort Pickens, Gulf Shores National Seashore

Rating: Beginner to Advanced

The first shots of the Civil War were fired on Santa Rosa Island, home to Fort Pickens. The fort was constructed to help defend Pensacola Pass and was the largest of the area forts. Geronimo was imprisoned here. In fact, for a time, viewing the Apache war chief became something of a local sideshow attraction. Today, the $8 fee to enter the park buys a valid pass for one week. The park offers fishing, camping, educational tours, and a small museum.

Beach lounging in Destin.

The place to snorkel is the jetties, which range from shore to about 50 feet deep. While snorkelers and swimmers are not allowed access to the waters around the pier, fishermen are allowed access to the jetties, and between boats, divers, and other snorkelers, the area can become congested. Tide is an important consideration when you are snorkeling here. Slack tide is the best time as the currents associated with a changing tide not only can be treacherous but also tend to muck up the visibility.

Sea urchins, crabs, and anemones can be found in the rocky crevices as well as a host of fish including sergeant majors, spadefish, and porcupine fish. Bottlenose dolphins, turtles, and rays also frequent the area.

Against an aging wooden fleet, the steel-hulled U.S.S. *Massachusetts* was a fully armored force to be reckoned with when she was launched in 1893. She saw action in the Spanish-American War. By World War I her construction had become antiquated and the ship was relegated to training missions. The 550-foot battleship, scuttled in 1921, lies in 20 plus feet of water 1 mile off the Fort Pickens jetties.

This site is best snorkeled at slack high or slack low tide because currents can become swift during the switch. Gun turrets from the U.S.S. *Massachusetts* stick up through the water's surface. Because of the currents and location, snorkelers can best visit this wreck when they are booked with a local charter boat.

Address: The end of Fort Pickens Road at the western end of Santa Rosa Island.

Directions: 9 miles west on Fort Pickens Road at the western end of Santa Rosa Island.

Hours of Operation: 8:00 a.m. to sundown, 365 days a year.

Visitor Information: 850.934.2600

Web site: www.nps.gov/guis

43

Destin Pass, Destin

Rating: Intermediate to Advanced

Look for the piles of rocks jutting into the water at the western tip of the peninsula. There are two sets of jetties: the main jetty and a smaller set of rocks 50 yards farther down the beach. Water depths range from 0 to 20 feet, depending on how far out you choose to swim. There is public access to the beach, though no public parking—the biggest problem with this site. Most people find an empty lot and park their car along the side of the road. As you drive onto the peninsula via Gulfshore Drive, try to park as close as you can to the second public beach access. The jetties are about a half-mile trek from there.

To fully appreciate the site, study the rock formations and natural caves for a number of different species of fish including gobies, damselfish, and snappers. The shells of fighting conchs are common, though they invariably house hermit crabs. Look for small flounder resting on top of the rocks. Because this is a highly trafficked area, dive flags are essential.

This site is recommended for intermediate snorkelers because the change of tide can create hazardous currents. The optimum time to visit this site is slack high tide, when visibility can reach as much as 40 feet. During the change of tide, the current will draw you down the jetty toward the pass and this can be dangerous, especially for those who are not confident swimmers.

Without a boat, there is no easy way to get to the jetty. It takes a lot of energy to walk down the beach to the snorkel site, dive in, and then walk all the way back down the beach to your car; this isn't a trip recommended for children or anyone not interested in working up a little sweat. Local snorkeling charters often include a

Destin Pass beach entrance.

trip to the jetties as one of the two sites typically visited on a charter. When you access the site with a local charter operation, the site becomes more family friendly.

Address: Gulfshore Drive.
Directions: From Hwy 98 heading west, turn left on Gulfshore
    Drive.
Hours of Operation: n/a
Visitor Information: n/a
Web site: n/a

44

St. Andrews State Recreational Park, Panama City

Rating: Beginner to Advanced

The park is 3 miles east of Panama City Beach and lined with one and a half miles of pristine water and sand. Like a great deal of Florida's Panhandle snorkeling destinations, often all it takes to find a site is to wade into the clear blue water and look around. Again, the general lack of structure can make species sighting sparse. The

Panama City Beach.

park is stunning, with rolling sand dunes, sea oats, and small trees. Restrooms and covered picnic facilities are available.

The best snorkeling can be done at the rock jetties. Crustaceans of all shapes, sizes, and colors call the cracks and crevices home, and in the summer months, when water temperatures reach the 80s, small colorful tropicals can be spotted. Conch and other intricately lined seashells are abundant along the seafloor. A fabulous snorkeling site for the whole family, the jetties are in 3 to 15 feet of water.

Plan to snorkel around the slack high tide as swift currents surrounding the change of tide make for dangerous swimming and murky viewing. Snorkeling equipment is available at the park. The park offers a shuttle service to nearby Shell Island, which is, for snorkelers and everyone else, a trip worth taking.

St. Andrews Beach, Panama City.

With 7 miles of beaches to wander, Shell Island was Dr. Beach's 1995 America's Best Beach winner. Though it stretches only three-quarters of a mile at its widest point, Shell Island supports a fresh-water swamp where alligators can be found. To see them doing what they normally do—lounging about sunning—follow one of the trails inland. Whatever your plans, pack cold drinks, snacks, sunscreen, and film as the island—accessible only by boat—offers no amenities.

Access to a boat shuttle can be obtained through the Jetty Store (850.233.0197); the shuttle departs from St. Andrews State Park every 30 minutes. Inquire as to the availability of snorkeling trips. The bay's seagrass beds are good shallow sites for any sized snorkeler. Starfish and scallops can be found in the seagrass, as well as little green grass shrimp and pipefish. The rock jetties at the entrance to the bay provide good structure for small tropicals, urchins, and game fish.

Dolphins have also been known to frequent this area. The waters here are home to some of the highest concentrations of bottle-nosed dolphins in the world. Social creatures, dolphins regularly swim right up to boats in the water. Should you plan to be on the Shell Island Shuttle, or any boat for that matter, have your camera ready.

Address: 4607 State Park Lane, Panama City.
Directions: From 98, south to Highway 3031, south to Highway 392.
Hours of Operation: 8:00 a.m. to sundown, 365 days a year.
Visitor Information: 850.233.5140
Web site: www.floridastateparks.org/standrews/

45

St. Joseph Peninsula State Park, Port St. Joe

Rating: Beginner to Advanced

With 17 miles of beaches, plenty of space makes Cape San Blas ideal for families. Snorkelers can hire a charter boat or simply stroll along the beach and explore the seagrass shallows at their own pace. For those who want to explore the cape, there are commercially undisturbed beaches open only to foot traffic. Boat charters last between three and four hours and will take you to specific locations that local captains recognize as friendly for snorkeling.

The bay water is perfect for the smallest snorkelers. The bay is calm, clear, and shallow. With little to no undertow, these beaches are considered some of the safest in the state. The seagrass beds flourishing along the bottom hide colorful scallops ripe for the picking—when in season. Scallop season runs from July through September 10.

Horseshoe crabs frequently patrol the grassy bottom like prehistoric army tanks traveling in reverse. Their label is a bit of a misnomer as horseshoe crabs are not crabs at all but, in fact, are related to scorpions. However, these relatives are completely harmless. The bay's seagrass beds also hide the crustaceans that sea turtles like to snack on, including lobster and crab. Consequently, visits by these graceful reptiles are not uncommon.

Address: 8899 Cape San Blas Road, St. Joe.
Directions: From Highway 98, heading east, State Road 30-A to State Road 30.
Hours: 8:00 a.m. to sundown, 365 days a year.
Visitor Information: 850.227.1327
Web site: www.floridastateparks.org/stjoseph/

Hawksbill turtle.

Chambers of Commerce

More information can be obtained from the following chambers of commerce:

Destin
4484 Legendary Dr.
850.837.6241
www.destinchamber.com

Panama City
235 W. 5th St.
850.785.5206
www.panamacity/org

Perdido Key
15500 Perdido Key Dr.
850.492.4660

Port St. Joe
155 Captain Fred's Place
850.227.1223
www.gulfchamber.org

Chapter 5

Southwest Coastline

Because of the sandy nature of the Gulf floor, the downside of snorkeling in this section of the state is the generally poor visibility. On a perfect day when the tide is high and slack and the sun is bright, visibility might reach 20 feet. In these waters in particular, slack high tide is the best time to snorkel. During the turn of the tide, bottom sediments stir and cloud the water. At slack tide, still waters give bottom sediments the chance to settle back to the seafloor.

Snorkeling in Florida.

Still, while Southwest Florida may not be the pearl of snorkeling in the Sunshine State, there is good snorkeling to be had in these waters. One of the best sites is Egmont Key, found at the mouth of Tampa Bay. Other sites include Venice, for the shark tooth collector in all of us, and Delnor-Wiggins Pass State Park where, on clear days, the shallows offshore will reveal small-profile corals.

For the most part, snorkelers will be exploring open seafloors dotted with an odd piece of structure, shallow ledge, or sandbar. When snorkeling over seagrass beds, be patient and keep a sharp eye out for baby boxfish, seahorses, and small invertebrates like crab and shrimp.

Above the Surface

Southwest Florida is stingray country. To avoid unwanted interactions with these docile creatures, the preferred mode of locomotion is the Stingray Shuffle. Rather than absently plodding along through the water, shuffle your feet across the sandy bottom as a means of alerting any stingray in the area to your presence; doing this will give any stingrays in the area ample opportunity to get out of your way. Nomadic creatures, stingrays can be spotted near coral reefs, seagrass beds, mangrove estuaries, and the sandy shallows close to shore. Shallow water does not deter these creatures and they can, in fact, be spotted in water less than one inch deep.

Southwest Florida is also home to one of the top manatee viewing areas in the Sunshine State. Manatees are attracted to the warm-water spill-off from the Florida Power and Electric plant on the Orange River in Fort Myers. Manatee Park is such a hot manatee spotting site that there is a Manatee Viewing Hotline (239.694.3537). To find the park from I-75, travel east to Exit 25, or State Road 80. The park is at 10901 State Road 80.

This area is really known for shelling. Sanibel and Captiva islands, in particular, are an absolute seashell paradise. Lightning whelks in pristine condition are as common as olives, scallops, murexes, and fighting conchs. The horse conch, Florida's state

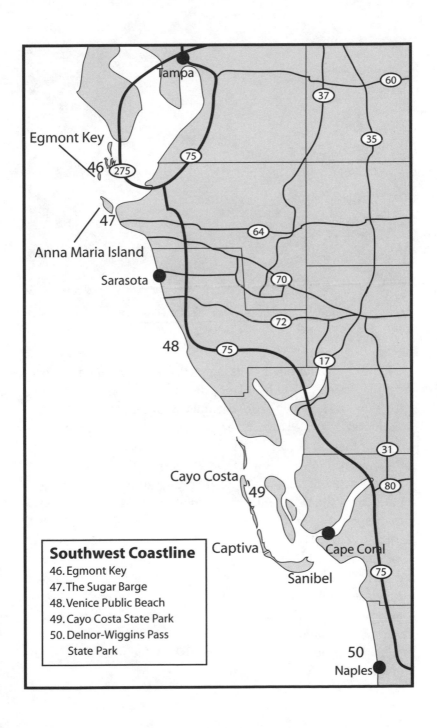

Egmont Key

46

47

Anna Maria Island

Sarasota

48

Cayo Costa

49

Captiva

Sanibel

Tampa

60

37

35

75

64

70

72

75

17

31

80

Cape Coral

75

50

Naples

Southwest Coastline
46. Egmont Key
47. The Sugar Barge
48. Venice Public Beach
49. Cayo Costa State Park
50. Delnor-Wiggins Pass
    State Park

The face of a mermaid?

shell, can be found in all of its stages, from the pumpkin-orange fingernail-sized shell of its infancy to the football-sized monster it grows up to be. The diversity of mollusk species native to Southwest Florida is rivaled only by the intricate designs and extravagant colors of their shells. To see the whole collection, visit the Bailey-Mathews Shell Museum on Sanibel Island.

The beaches of Sanibel and neighboring Captiva Island, in fact, rank among the top shelling beaches in the world. Where some beaches are covered in sand, these beaches are literally covered in seashells. Shell collecting is serious business in these parts, and residents and visitors alike can be found combing the beaches at first light. The shell collector's familiar pose, bending down to poke a finger at a shell, is known locally as the Sanibel Stoop. Snorkelers can get a leg up on Sanibel Stoopers by patrolling the shallows just offshore. The bottom is loaded with shells waiting their turn to wash up to shore. Collecting live shells—including starfish, sand dollars, and sea urchins—is prohibited.

46

Egmont Key State Park, Tampa Bay

Rating: Beginner to Advanced

Fort Dade, on Egmont Key, was built in 1882 to help defend Tampa during the Spanish-American War. The Spanish never did threaten the city, and the fort's inhabitants left years ago. Today, the tiny island houses a healthy colony of gopher tortoises. Spend at least some time exploring the fort by foot. The island is accessible only by boat, and on the ride out, your captain will likely promise that dolphins will swim up to the boat and jump in the wake. Have your camera ready! There are no concessions on the island and you'll want to pack out everything you pack in. Egmont Key State Park may represent the best snorkeling in the area.

Two snorkeling experiences are accessible. The first is over some of the structural remains of the fort that have fallen into the water; snapper, small tropicals, crabs, and sea urchins gather here. The other choice is over the seagrass beds, where starfish, rays, conchs, and a host of other species can sometimes be found.

Stroll along the oceanside beaches for an impressive display of seashells. No live shells should be taken, including starfish, sand dollars, and sea urchins. Be careful of shells housing hermit crabs. To make sure a shell is indeed empty, set it down on the sand for a minute and then wait to see if it starts to crawl away.

To reach Egmont Key, a number of local charters offer daily service and snorkeling packages. A ferry runs from Clearwater's Fort DeSoto County Park twice a day. The ferry does not always run, so call ahead to make sure (727.867.6569). Generally, the ferry leaves at 10 a.m. and 11 a.m. and then heads out to pick people up at 2 p.m. and 3 p.m.

Address: Island, accessible only by boat.

Directions: At the mouth of Tampa Bay, southwest of Fort Desoto Beach.

Hours of Operation: 8:00 a.m. to sundown, 365 days a year.

Visitor Information: 727.893.2627

Web site: www.floridastateparks.org/egmontkey/

47

The Sugar Barge, Anna Maria Island

Rating: Intermediate to Advanced

The Sugar Barge Wreck, also called the *Regina*, like the *Urca de Lima*, the *San Pedro*, and the U.S.S. *Massachusetts*, are all part of Florida's historic Shipwreck Trail. The *Regina* was carrying a load of molasses when the 247-foot tanker was pushed aground by high winds and heavy surf off Anna Maria Island in 1940. The corner of Gulf Drive and 7th Street roughly marks the longitude of the wreck.

The ship is in 20 feet of water approximately 75 yards from the beach. Dive flags are essential. Some of the wreckage is only 6 or so feet beneath the surface, and snorkeling at slack low tide can make locating the ship easier. Because of the depth of the wreck and its distance offshore, this is a site recommended for more advanced snorkelers.

In this area of the state especially, it is important to snorkel at slack tide, and preferably slack high tide. Slack tide will produce the best possible snorkeling environment. A good time to go is early in the morning before the wind begins to pick up and create choppy water. Sunny days with direct light will increase the visibility in the water while cloudy, shady days will decrease it.

Address: South end of Anna Maria Island at Gulf Drive and 7th Street.
Directions: From I-75, Exit 220, heading west, Route 64 becomes Manatee Avenue.
Hours of Operation: n/a
Visitor Information: n/a
Web site: n/a

48

Venice Public Beach, Venice

Rating: Beginner to Advanced

Venice Public Beach, in the heart of downtown Venice, is a lovely stretch of beach perfect for lounging. It has ample public parking, restroom facilities, a playground, lifeguards, and plenty of nearby shopping. Venice is known as the "Shark Tooth Capital of the World" as the waters and beaches are littered with fossilized shark's teeth.

Unfurl your towel on the beach; take your mask, snorkel, fins, and dive flag to the edge of the water, and wade in. This is snorkeling with a mission. There is not a lot of marine life to see, maybe a stingray or occasional starfish, but there are loads of shark teeth to find. Patrol the shallows close to shore. It takes patience to find them, and this is not a passive activity. The teeth are often buried beneath a layer of silt. Gently waving your hand back and forth over the sand will displace the top layer of silt and sometimes reveal a shark's tooth. This activity will also cloud the water and worsen visibility. Should there be a current, work against it. Another way to find teeth is to use a small dip net or a strainer to sift through the sand. This works both on the beach and in the water.

Farther off the beach, where the water is 15 to 18 feet deep, snorkelers have the chance to find fossilized teeth as big as a baby's hand. Again, this is not snorkeling for beginners, and finding teeth has a fairly high degree of luck attached to it. Beginning snorkelers will want to try their hand closer to shore.

The teeth can be found on all the beaches in the area, not just the Venice Public Beach. Minutes north of Venice on U.S. 41, the beaches of Nokomis and Casey Key are similarly loaded. Because the bigger teeth have yet to wash ashore, finding them requires patrolling the bottom offshore where they have been buried beneath the silt.

Address: West Venice Avenue.
Directions: I-75 to Jacaranda Blvd., west on Venice Avenue.
Hours of Operation: n/a
Visitor Information: n/a
Web site: n/a

49

Cayo Costa State Park, Pine Island Sound

Rating: Beginner to Advanced

Florida's barrier islands are some of the state's most breathtaking assets, and Cayo Costa is no exception. The island is protected by the state, and its beauty is uncompromised by commercial development. Relatively uninhabited, it has limited camping sites for those with tents. Twelve rustic cabins are also available.

The *Tropic Star* of Pine Island (239.283.0015) provides ferry service to Cayo Costa twice daily. Reservations are required. The island can also be reached by kayak from Pine Island. Florida's other state bird, the mosquito, is rampant on the island, as is the infrequently seen—though often felt—noseeum. When you visit the island, be sure to take bug repellent. There are no amenities on the island, and visitors are expected to pack in what they need, and pack out what they use.

Like most of the snorkeling sites along this part of the coast, the snorkeling is hit and miss because of the area's propensity for poor visibility. Cayo Costa is, however, one of the primary snorkeling destinations for charter boat captains working out of the Cape Coral, Fort Myers, and Pine Island areas. While the snorkeling will not compare to the snorkeling in other parts of the state, the water is by no means devoid of life. The luck of being in the right place at the right time, more than anything else, is what snorkelers should hope for.

With no corals to provide structure, snorkelers patrol the shallows in search of ledges, sponges, and debris where fish will gather. Seashells and sand dollars will definitely be on the snorkeling menu. On that note, do not leave without strolling along the beach because, unlike Sanibel and Captiva, Cayo Costa beaches are not routinely picked clean of seashells. Remember, live shelling, including conch and starfish, is prohibited.

Assortment of seashells found on Sanibel.

Any trip to Cayo Costa should include a stop at Cabbage Key for a cold beer and a cheeseburger. These are not the cheeseburgers Jimmy Buffett sings about in one particular song, though you will undoubtedly hear assertions of this claim. The inspiration for Buffett's burgers was found in the Tortolos. Do not expect filet mignon, except from the atmosphere. Cabbage Key is more like a margarita-drenched song that drifts across as ceiling fans spin hopelessly against the heat. Dollar bills signed in black and red ink are taped to every open inch of wall space. Hotel accommodations are available.

Address: Island, accessible by boat only.
Directions: Just south of Boca Grande.
Hours of Operation: 8:00 a.m. to sundown, 365 days a year.
Visitor Information: 941.964.0375
Web site: www.floridastateparks.org/cayocosta/

50

Delnor-Wiggins Pass State Park, Naples

Rating: Intermediate to Advanced

Though occupied by Calusa and Seminole Indians since the 1600s, the pass is named for Joe Wiggins, an early homesteader who operated a small trading post in the area. Heading south, Delnor-Wiggins is the last best place to snorkel on Florida's west coast. Along with a mile-long stretch of white sandy beach, there is a hard-bottom coral community in the shallows 200 feet or so from the beach. Bathrooms, showers, and picnic facilities are available.

On clear, calm days at slack high tide, you can see small tropicals and low-profile stony and soft corals. The best time to snorkel this site is when the sun is high and there is little to no breeze chopping at the surface. For snorkeling purposes, park in Lot 2 at the southern end of the park near the ranger station, walk out to the beach, don your mask and fins, and wade out into the water.

During turtle nesting season, park rangers offer a sea turtle program on Friday mornings that gives participants the chance to stroll the beach in hopes of identifying fresh turtle tracks and newly dug nests.

For orchid lovers, the "Orchid Capital of Continental North America" is close by. Forty-four native orchids, including the breathtakingly beautiful ghost orchid, grow in Fakahatchee Strand Preserve State Park. South of Naples—take State Road 29 south from the small town of Copeland—the park is on Janes Memorial Scenic Drive. The Fakahatchee Strand is a thin slice of swamp forest; from November through February, park rangers lead guided swamp walks through waist-deep water. Guided canoe trips are also available. Space on these trips is limited, and you need to make reservations in advance. For those who are interested in learning more, the phone number is 239.695.4593.

Address: 1100 Gulfshore Drive, Naples.

Directions: From I-75, take Exit 111 west for 6 miles.

Hours of Operation: 8:00 a.m. to sundown, 365 days a year.

Visitor Information: 239.597.6196

Web site: www.floridastateparks.org/delnor-wiggins/

Delnor-Wiggins Pass beach.

Chambers of Commerce

More information can be obtained from the following chambers of commerce:

Anna Maria Island Chamber of Commerce
9313 Gulf Drive N.
941.778.1541
www.annamariaislandchamber.org

Fort Myers
2310 Edwards Drive
239.332.3624
www.fortmyers.org

Naples
2390 Tamiami Trail
239.262.6141
www.napleschamber.org

Sanibel-Captiva
1159 Causeway Road
239.472.1080
www.sanibel-captiva.org

Venice
597 Tamiami Trail
941.488.2236
www.venicechamber.com

Part II

Preparations and Precautions

Watch for warning flags on local beaches.

Chapter 6

Worrisome Creatures

Jagged-toothed species like sharks, barracudas, and alligators are probably the first of the worrisome aquatic creatures to come to mind. However, the odds of having a negative encounter with one of these are astronomically low. If there is sea life you might have a negative encounter with, it will likely be jellyfish, sea lice, and mosquitoes! If any of these find you, reach for a tube of Cortisone or Benadryl and apply the cream to the affected area. Both ease minor itches and burns. These creams also work wonders for burns associated with fire coral and fire worms.

Jellyfish

The rule of thumb with jellyfish is that the longer the tentacle is, the more painful the sting will be. The Portuguese man-o-war, one of Florida's most potent jellyfish, has tentacles that can stretch out more than 150 feet. Jellyfish use their tentacles for hunting much like a spider uses its web. The prey on which jellyfish feed are first paralyzed and then entangled by the tentacle mass. The tentacles are laced with tiny hair-triggered stinging cells called nematocysts—mindless stingers activated by touch.

Unfortunately, from time to time people become caught in these webs. This is not a fatal condition, and should it happen, do not rinse the area with fresh water as it will activate unreleased nematocysts. Rinse with seawater. Do not rub the affected area as contact will further activate nematocysts. Pick off lingering tentacles with gloves or tweezers. If vinegar or isopropyl alcohol is available, pouring either over the affected area will help to neutralize any remaining stinging cells.

Contrary to popular myth, the only benefit gained from urinating on a jellyfish sting is relief of a bladder. Sprinkling meat tenderizer over the area will help to neutralize the venom and soaking the sting in hot water will lessen the pain.

Portuguese man-o-war are wind-blown creatures that are often pushed right into shore. Deceptively pretty, the balloon of the man-o-war is ringed with beautiful blue and pink shades that may prove especially attractive to children. Remember that a jellyfish's nematocysts are activated by touch, and even though a jellyfish has washed ashore, it is still capable of delivering a sting.

Sea Lice

Sea lice are larval jellyfish and cause skin irritations including rashes and welts. Especially prevalent along Florida's east coast and around the Keys, sea lice season runs from March to August. Heeding posted warning signs and staying out of the water during particularly heavy sea lice infestation can help you avoid a great deal of discomfort. Because they are so small, sea lice get trapped in clothing and the friction of rubbing against the skin causes their nematocysts to fire. Sea lice are just as likely to be encountered on the reef as they are in the shallows off the beach.

Fire Coral

Fire coral is a species that can be hard to identify—until you've brushed up against it and discovered it the hard way. Fire coral can look both sponge-like and coralesque. It is polymorphic by nature and grows over already existing structures like dead corals and sponges. Fire coral can appear branched or fanned and can be light brown to mustard in color. What most fire corals have in common is that the tips of their structures are whitish. Fire coral is carpeted with nematocysts, the same hair-trigger stinging cells that arm jellyfish. The sting is mild, though irritating, and you will know if you brush accidentally against it. Fire coral grows in almost any marine environment, from dock pilings and rocky inshore bottoms to off-shore wrecks and reefs.

Fire Worms

Fire worms are often referred to as bristle worms. Both are seg-mented worms looking somewhat like a centipede, only they have white puffy tufts like epaulets sprouting from their bodies. These white tufts are filled with nematocysts—the same hair-trigger stinging cells arming jellyfish and fire coral. Most common in the Keys and along the southeast coast of Florida, fire worms occur from the coastline to the reefs. Should you, for some odd reason, reach out and touch one of these, soaking the affected area in hot water will help to lessen the pain.

Sea Urchins

Sea urchins inhabit inshore seagrass shallows, sponge beds, and rocky terrain as well as the nooks and crannies of coral reefs. Sea urchins are a sort of maintenance crew for the reefs. Like prickly lawnmowers, they make their living grazing algae from the cor-als. Left unattended, algae would grow rampant and suffocate the corals.

The sea urchin is the pincushion of the sea. Unmistakable in appearance, the urchins can prick you the wrong way should you reach out and touch one. The needle-like quills will pierce your skin like a warm knife slicing butter and then deliver a poisonous but mild sting. Should you have an encounter with one of these quills, use hot water and cortisone cream to lessen any discom-fort.

Scorpionfish

Scorpionfish are ugly little brutes and perfect reasons not to reach out and touch the reefs when you are snorkeling. Brilliantly camouflaged, a scorpionfish does not appear to be resting on the rocks but rather seems to be just another piece of rock. Scorpionfish lie waiting for smaller, tastier fish to swim by oblivious to them; the scorpionfish gulps them down. Scorpionfish come equipped with three poison-filled barbs that, when touched, can elicit a pretty intense—though certainly not fatal—sting. Not commonly found inshore, scorpionfish prefer to rest in rocky areas and on and around reefs.

Stingrays

The southern stingray (Plate 12) is one of the most common species of rays found in Florida. This kite-shaped ray is brown in color and possesses a long, whip-like tail. Stingrays can be found in waters only two inches deep as they patrol the bottom in search of crabs, shrimp, and other stingray delicacies. They also bury themselves in the sand and wait for unsuspecting meals to scurry by. This is generally the time when stingrays and people interact. The stingray is buried in the sand and when someone walks through the water and steps on it, in an attempt to defend itself, the stingray will whip its tail at the aggressor. The tail is armed with a jagged stinger capable of injecting a painful but not lethal poison.

Stingrays are nonaggressive and will not attack you, but they will react to being stepped on or grabbed. Not stepping on them can be accomplished by doing the Stingray Shuffle. Instead of plodding through the water, shuffle your feet along the bottom. Shuffling announces your approach to the stingray and allows it ample time to get out of the way.

Sharks

Florida takes a particularly bad rap for its sharks; they are not predatory monsters. While shark attacks do occur, snorkelers should remember that the odds of one happening to them are astronomically low. According to the Florida Museum of Natural History's International Shark Attack Files, between 1911 and 2005, there were

483 reported unprovoked attacks in Florida waters. That may seem like a large number, but snorkelers can take comfort in knowing that over 300 of the 483 attacks occurred in waters well north of any snorkeling site listed in this book!

In any case, divide the number of reported shark attacks in the last century by the millions of swimmers splashing around daily in coastal waters and you will see that, statistically, snorkelers are more likely to be struck on the head by a falling coconut than they are to be attacked by a shark. So unless you are afraid of getting bonked on the head by a coconut, grab your snorkel, your mask, and your sense of adventure and prepare to discover some of Florida's most brilliant snorkeling.

The good news is that sharks do not consider people food. The bad news is that they don't have fingers. In order to gather tactile information they have to use their mouths. Because of this, the most common kind of shark attack is called a hit and run. In this case, the shark takes one bite to see if the object is a food source, and finding in the case of humans that it is not, it swims away. This is why there have been fewer than 15 shark-related deaths in Florida waters over the last 100 years.

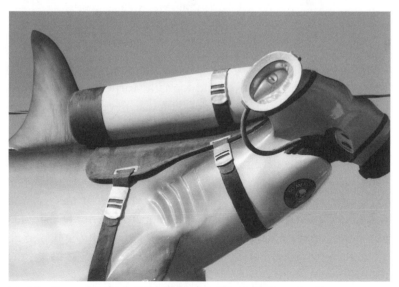

Look for the scuba shark at Whale Harbor, Upper Matecumbe Key.

An inordinately high number of shark attacks in Florida are retaliatory strikes against a human aggressor. Believe it or not, nurse sharks account for a percentage of reported shark attacks. Wait a minute. Nurse sharks are docile and rarely appear interested in snorkelers swimming by. Sometimes, however, brilliant people reach down and grab them by the tail. Surprisingly, the shark turns around and bites!

Sharks are evolutionary marvels and have been around since before fish first crawled out of the sea. In the unlikely event that you encounter a shark while snorkeling, do your best to stay calm. Erratic movements, including pounding hearts, can attract further interest from the shark. Remember that sharks are a curious species and not mindless hunters.

Steps can be taken to minimize the chance of unwanted shark encounters. Always snorkel with a buddy. Avoid murky water and river mouths. Don't snorkel at night or early evening when sharks are most active. And last, do not snorkel with open wounds that are bleeding. Blood is the number one attractant to sharks. To put all of this shark chatter into perspective, you are much more likely to be struck by lightning, to be swarmed by bees, to be attacked by a dog, or to win the lottery than to be attacked by a shark.

Barracuda

Barracuda are big and silver and look like torpedoes. Adults can travel in packs and scan the water with black eyes as big as quarters. These fish have wicked, pointy-toothed grins, and it is suggested that a barracuda will strike when it mistakes the flash of sunlight reflecting off a piece of jewelry for the sunlight flash off a fish's scales. Though the odds of this happening barely register, just to be safe, snorkel without jewelry. Barracuda are curious fish and will follow quietly behind you. If this happens, do not feel singled out—it is common barracuda behavior. If you want the fish to go away, turning around and slowly swim toward it. Most likely, the fish will swim away.

Eels

Eels consider coral reefs favorable housing. Spotted eels and green moray eels are two of the more prevalent Florida species. While neither frequents inshore communities, remember that none of these rules are hard and fast. Eels are like underwater snakes with flat tails. When unmolested, eels, like strangers, pets, and most wild creatures, go about their day-to-day business without giving much care to passersby. Though few eel bites are reported each year, like nurse sharks, a good many involve a retaliatory strike against a human aggressor. Should you choose to tug on the tail of a free-swimming eel, or if you stick your fingers into prime eel habitat such as cracks, crevices, and holes, do not be surprised at the result.

Mosquitoes and Noseeums

Mosquitoes love warm and moist environments, so they thrive in Florida. They are also natural-born snorkelers and, as larvae, wriggle beneath the water and breathe through small snorkeling tubes. You don't have to worry about the males. The females of the species are the bloodthirsty ones and brazenly feed on the warm-blooded. Body heat attracts them. The unfortunate truth is that there is just no way to avoid the mosquito. In fact, there are some people who consider the mosquito to be Florida's state bird. Funny, yes. Accurate, no. The state bird is the mockingbird.

As for chemical repellents, those containing DEET are widely considered the most effective. Some people say citronella works. Some people burn charcoal or incense. What works for some will not work for others. In the end, the cold hard truth is that mosquitoes find some people more succulent than others.

They are, however, only half the problem. Florida also has a species of insect it calls noseeums. Pronounced no-see-ums, these are tiny biting flies actually called midges. Easily mistaken for an innocuous speck of dirt, what a noseeum lacks in size it certainly makes up for in bite. Like mosquitoes, noseeums are most active in the late afternoon and evening. To help alleviate the itch, cortisone cream can, once again, feel like a lifesaver.

Alligators

Do not feed alligators. Alligators are dangerous. Feeding them makes them more so. The alligator that associates people with food is not only the most brazen but also the most dangerous of all. Alligators are freshwater reptiles and can be found in canals, ponds, lakes, rivers, and occasionally, backyard swimming pools. Alligators are most active, and most aggressive, during their mating season—roughly April to June—when both the weather and the water begin to heat up.

Whenever you are snorkeling in fresh water, be aware of your surroundings. For snorkelers concerned with being attacked by an alligator, like shark attacks, swarms of bees, winning lottery tickets, and killer coconuts, the odds of it happening to you are unlikely. The family member most likely to suffer an attack is Spot or Fluffy. Be cautious when pets begin sniffing at the edges of ponds, creeks, lakes, and rivers. To see an alligator lying in the sun, you might easily get the impression these are slow and lazy beasts. These reptiles are cunning predators capable of striking with stealth, force, and speed. Respect alligators, and give them a wide berth.

American alligator in Everglades National Park.

Chapter 7

Essentials

~~~~~~

The very least you need to have a great time snorkeling is a snorkel, a mask, fins, and a body of water deep enough to float in. First-timers should know that with the wrong equipment—mostly a leaky mask—snorkeling can be a frustrating experience. Some basic knowledge of snorkeling equipment will help to improve your experience (Plate 13).

Snorkeling equipment is pretty basic stuff and does not require a tremendous financial investment. For those planning on signing up with a snorkeling charter, you won't even have to worry about this. In most cases, you will be able to rent the equipment at the dock. Some parks also have equipment available for rental.

For those who do not want to buy their own gear but would like to have it available for a long weekend or even a week, many scuba diving shops have rental equipment available. While snorkels, masks, and fins are the snorkeling essentials, they are not the end of the story. Safety vests and Diver Down flags are valuable, and often necessary, tools.

Snorkels

There is nothing natural about putting your face in the water and breathing through a tube, and for some it can be uncomfortable. Fortunately, the skill can be mastered in as few as two short breaths. It may be prudent to get used to breathing through a snorkel before diving in. Stick the snorkel in your mouth and walk around your bedroom. Jump in a swimming pool and practice breathing.

There are four kinds of snorkels: the basic J-tube snorkel, the purge snorkel, the dry snorkel, and the specialty snorkels like the radio snorkel that has an FM radio embedded into the mouthpiece. Strip away the bells and whistles and all of them involve a breathing tube and a mouthpiece.

A basic snorkel lets you breathe; purge snorkels come equipped with a purging device to remove water from the breathing tube; and dry snorkels are designed to keep water from entering the tube altogether. However, snorkeling is a wet activity and invariably water will get inside the tube. When this happens, a strong exhalation at the surface will blow out any water in the tube. One technique for doing this is to place your tongue on the roof of your mouth and make a forceful "T" sound—or you can just blow. After clearing the tube, your next breath should be a cautionary one in case there is residual water still in the tube.

The most important feature of a snorkel is its mouthpiece. Make sure the snorkel you choose fits comfortably inside your mouth. As all mouths are slightly different in shape and size, so are mouthpieces. Should a mouthpiece feel too wide or too hard, try another brand, or purchase a replacement mouthpiece for your gear. Once you are snorkeling, try to remember that it is unnecessary to chomp down on the mouthpiece. The natural seal created by your lips will keep the water out. Chomping down on the mouthpiece will only lead to a sore jaw.

Masks

An ill-fitting mask can make or break your snorkeling experience. Like the mouthpiece, not all masks are designed exactly the same. Some masks are designed for people with broader faces, and some are designed for people with narrower faces. When picking out a mask, you should look for three things: a mask that delivers a good field of vision, does not pinch or squeeze around the nose or on the forehead, and doesn't leak.

To test whether a mask fits your face, perform these steps: fold the strap over the lens, put the mask against your face, inhale through your nose, and let go. If an airtight seal forms, the mask will stick to your face. If it slips off, there is no airtight seal, and once in the water, the mask will leak. Pick another mask and repeat the process until you find one that properly fits your face.

Before using a new mask for the first time, you will need to clean the lens. Manufacturers apply protective oil to the lens that needs to be removed; otherwise, your mask will likely fog. Toothpaste, dishwashing detergent, and shampoo are all excellent cleaning agents. Apply to the inside of the lens, scrub with your fingertips, and rinse. Repeat. This will not be the last time you scrub the lens of your mask with your fingertips. The next time, you will likely be using your own saliva.

A thin film of saliva on the inside lens of your mask will help impede water droplets from beading up in your mask and obscuring your vision. Some people's saliva seems to work better than others and if, for whatever reason, yours is not doing the job, you can apply an antifogging solution. These solutions can be purchased at any dive store and are applied in the same way as saliva. Place a few drops on your lens, spread around with your fingers, and rinse. Rinse twice. If the solution is not thoroughly rinsed from the mask and gets into your eyes, like sunscreen lotion, it is going to burn.

The big issue with masks is leaking. Leaks can be caused by a number of things, even with properly fitted masks. Pulling the strap too tightly around your head can cause the skirt of the mask to buckle and break the airtight seal around your face. Smiling causes your skin to crease, which also compromises the skirt's seal. Facial hair causes leaks, and for those with beards or moustaches, spreading a petroleum-based jelly around the hairline will plug any gaps in the seal.

Should you, however, be on the boat—or worse, in the water—and find yourself wrestling with a leaky mask, lip balm or petroleum lubricants can seal the problem. For temporary relief, smearing either one liberally over the skin where it comes into contact with the leaky part of the mask should help to plug any leaks.

For people with long, thick, or curly hair, the mask's factory-issued strap can tangle and pull at your hair. Replacing the strap

Snorkelers searching for manatees in the Kings River.

with a neoprene head strap will usually solve this problem. And, as a last note, for those who use corrective lenses for day-to-day living, masks can be custom-fitted with a lens that matches your prescription.

Fins

The bottom line on fins is that anything is better than nothing. Like mouthpieces and masks, they should feel comfortable—snug, but not so snug as to cut off your blood circulation. Fins come in two styles: open-heel and closed-heel. Closed-heel fins are often lighter than open-heel fins, perfect for snorkeling and generally less expensive than open-heel fins. Open-heel fins are generally bulkier, preferred by scuba divers, and require you to wear neoprene socks called booties. Should blistering be a problem when you wear closed-heel fins, try wearing neoprene booties or even a pair of socks to keep the rubbing to a minimum.

Charter Boats

If you want to experience the coral reefs and sunken ships found offshore, getting to your favorite Florida snorkeling destination is never difficult, as finding a snorkeling charter is about as hard as finding something cold to drink. The best place to find a list of the area's available snorkeling charters is the local Chamber of Commerce; visit either online before your trip or in person when you reach your destination. Both the physical and online addresses of pertinent Chambers of Commerce are provided at the end of each section.

Typically, charter boats offer the same basic operation; they visit two sites and spend about 45 minutes at each location. Most charters operate twice a day once in the morning and once in the early afternoon. The biggest differences between charter boat operations are how many people the boat accommodates and where the captain takes you.

Charter boats come in three sizes: small, medium, and large. The smallest charters often accommodate fewer than six people; medium-sized charters can have as many as 20 snorkelers on board; and head boats, also called cattle boats, offer snorkeling trips for as many as 100 people. While these will often be the most affordable trips, that many bodies splashing into the water at one time can detract from your snorkeling experience.

Snorkeling is thirsty business, and any charter boat worth its salt will provide fresh water. Many charter boat operations offer juice or sodas after a snorkel. In Key West, some captains offer beer and wine. In any case, the boat should have an ice chest on board where it is perfectly acceptable to stow snacks or beverages. When boarding with these, just ask the captain or mate where to put them. Fruits like sliced oranges, apples, and melons are refreshing after a swim. Bananas, however, are frowned upon by sailors, who are a superstitious lot. While great sources of nutrition, bananas are considered bad luck, and they are unwelcome on most boats.

Seasickness

For those susceptible to the ill effects of motion, few things are worse than getting seasick. Rest assured, once you get in the water, you won't be seasick any more. However, after the symptoms arrive, it is too late for antiemetic pills like Dramamine or Bonne to be effective. These need to be taken at least one hour before a scheduled trip, and they remain effective for about four hours. Your doctor can write you a prescription for a seasickness patch that can work for as long as three days.

For thousands of years, Chinese sailors have chewed ginger root to cure seasickness. Ingesting ginger increases the output of the digestive fluids that neutralize rising stomach acids. The best last-ditch effort, short of abandoning ship, is ingesting some ginger-related product like ginger ale, ginger beer, or pickled ginger (the kind served with sushi).

Safety Vests

As a precaution, you should also wear snorkeling safety vests—especially if you are venturing offshore or are uncomfortable in the water. Safety vests are inflatable life jackets and come in both adult and children's sizes. Equipped with a flexible manual inflation tube, the vest can be quickly deflated when you dive into the water and quickly reinflated when you return to the surface. These vests do not require huffing and puffing to inflate. Two or three breaths will be enough to keep you afloat. There is no law dictating that every snorkeler has to wear a safety vest, but it is always a good idea—and generally insisted upon by snorkeling charter captains and crew.

Diver Down Flags

With your buddy in tow and your safety vest secured, unless you are snorkeling in a roped-off boater-free zone, you had better have a dive flag. In Florida, state law dictates that snorkelers display a Diver Down flag when they are in the water. On seeing the internationally recognized red and white striped flag, passing boaters are required to remain a minimum of 100 feet away while inshore and 300 feet away from any flag spotted offshore. Boaters are also required to maintain an idle speed while within 300 feet of a Diver Down flag.

The flags can be displayed from a boat, or from a buoy that is attached to the snorkeler by a leash. In either case, the flag must be sufficiently raised as to be visible from all directions. Diver Down flags attached to boats are to measure a minimum of 20" x 24". Flags attached to leashed buoys should measure at least 12" x 12". Failure to fly a flag will not only inhibit the ability of passing boaters to be aware that snorkelers are in the water, but it is also reason for the Florida Marine Patrol to issue a citation.

Spearfishing

For those interested in spearfishing, be advised that it is not allowed in Collier County or in Monroe County (the Keys) from Long Key north to the Dade County line. Statewide, spearfishing is not permitted within 100 yards of a public beach, 100 yards of a commercial or public fishing pier, 100 yards of any portion of bridge where pole fishing is legally permitted, or 100 feet of a submerged portion of jetty unless the structure juts out more than 1,500 yards from shore; in the last case, spearfishing is permitted within the last 500 yards of the jetty. National Parks and Marine Sanctuaries are always off limits. Using power heads and bang sticks is illegal. Depending on the species, all rules and regulations regarding size and season apply. A Florida fishing license is required.

The following species are considered illegal kills for spearfishing: billfish, sturgeon, tarpon, bonefish, Goliath grouper, Nassau grouper, permit, pompano, African pompano, shark, spotted eagle ray (Plate 14), manta ray, snook, red drum (redfish), spotted sea trout, weakfish, tripletail, surgeonfish, trumpetfish, angelfish (Plate 15), damselfish, butterflyfish, porcupinefish, cornetfish, squirrelfish, trunkfish, parrotfish, pipefish, seahorse, lobster, and puffers (Plate 16).

Acknowledgments

~~~~~~

Thank you for your belief, trust, and support: David Earle, Meredith Morris-Babb, John Byram, Amy Gorelick, Sandi Newman, and Micky Morrison. And to my family: Michelle Zemo, Judy Sills, Dennis Carroll, and Noel and Pat Bertelli.

Credits

All images are from the author's personal collection except for the following, which were generously loaned by those credited.

Leon Behar: Plate 9, mermaid with manatee

M. Morrison: Plate 3, pork fish; Plate 7, nurse shark; Plate 11, Atlantic spadefish; Plate 14, spotted eagle ray

P. Taylor: Plate 1, queen angelfish; Plate 5, Christmas tree worms; Plate 6, hogfish; Plate 15, queen angelfish; Plate 16, pufferfish; Plate 12, southern stingray; Plate 13, sea rods

The Turtle Hospital: Turtle Hospital ambulance (page 14); Plate 2, *Fibropapilloma*

M. Zemo: Destin Pass beach entrance (page 116)

Index

Brad Bertelli is an award-winning writer who lives in the Florida Keys. An avid snorkeler, he has written about pirates, sunken treasures, and coral husbandry as a staff writer for the *Florida Scuba News*.